Coaches Marketing Roadmap

Accelerate your journey to a thriving coaching business.

By Cathy Smith

Foreword by Dale Beaumont

First published by Ultimate World Publishing 2024
Copyright © 2024 Cathy Smith

ISBN

Paperback: 978-1-923123-33-5
Ebook: 978-1-923123-34-2

Cathy Smith has asserted her rights under the Copyright, Designs and Patents Act 1988 to be identified as the author of this work. The information in this book is based on the author's experiences and opinions. The publisher specifically disclaims responsibility for any adverse consequences which may result from use of the information contained herein. Permission to use information has been sought by the author. Any breaches will be rectified in further editions of the book.

All rights reserved. No part of this publication may be reproduced, stored in or introduced into a retrieval system, or transmitted in any form, or by any means (electronic, mechanical, photocopying, recording or otherwise) without the prior written permission of the author. Any person who does any unauthorised act in relation to this publication may be liable to criminal prosecution and civil claims for damages. Enquiries should be made through the publisher.

Cover design: Cathy Smith
Layout and typesetting: Ultimate World Publishing
Editor: Marnae Kelley

Ultimate World Publishing
Diamond Creek,
Victoria Australia 3089
www.writeabook.com.au

Disclaimer

Please note that the *Coaches Marketing Roadmap* book is specially designed for a diverse range of professionals in the coaching industry, encompassing life, business, and wellness coaches. This comprehensive guide is crafted to support those who are looking to transform their coaching passion into a thriving business.

It is important to understand that this resource is NOT aimed at sports coaches.

The stories and examples contained in this book are based on true events and factual accounts. However, to protect the privacy and confidentiality of the individuals involved, all names and identifying details have been altered. Any resemblance to actual persons, living or dead, is purely coincidental. The intent of this work is not to defame or harm anyone but to offer insights and perspectives. Reader discretion is advised.

Whether you identify as a life coach, business coach, financial coach, spiritual coach, or any other form of personal or professional development coach, this book is for you.

Please enjoy.

Dedication

To my Husband and family. You are my why.

Contents

Disclaimer	iii
Dedication	v
Foreword	1
Introduction	5
Chapter 1: How to Stand Out on the Coaching Map	7
Chapter 2: Crafting an Identity Beyond the Certificate	19
Chapter 3: Turning Identity into a Brand	35
Chapter 4: Your Powerful Coaching Toolbox	47
Chapter 5: Setting Your Price for Success	57
Chapter 6: Laying the Groundwork to Attract Your Ideal Audience	69
Chapter 7: Marketing Magic to Find Clients Who Love You	83
Chapter 8: Magnetising Your Ideal Client	93
Chapter 9: Mastering the Art of Client Conversion	107
Chapter 10: Turning "No" Into "Yes" for Client Success	121
Chapter 11: Balancing Your Coaching Life for Long Term Success	131
Chapter 12: Your Roadmap to Mapping a Thriving Coaching Business	143
About the Author	151
Testimonials	153
Speaker Bio	155
Acknowledgements	157

Foreword

In 1998, when I was 17, I found myself seated in my career advisor's office. He began the meeting by asking, "So, son, what university are you going to when you finish school?"

To that, I answered, "I'm sorry sir, but I decided I'm not going to university."

He replied, "Why not?"

"Because what I want to be when I grow up is not actually a course at university."

"Well, what do you want to be?"

And I said, "I want to be a life coach, sir."

Bewildered, he questioned, "What the hell is a life coach?"

This initiated my explanation: a life coach, much like a personal trainer, guides individuals not only in physical health but also mental health, emotional well-being, relationships, finances—essentially anything they wish to succeed in—and the life coach facilitates their journey in the shortest time possible.

After this explanation, he said, "Well, sounds like you have given this a lot of thought. I wish you the best with this unusual career. If it doesn't work out, you can always go back to university." And that was the end of our meeting.

Fast forward to 2023, 25 years later. I'm pleased to say that I did become a life coach, and it has been a wonderful and successful career for me. I have gone onto earn almost $100 million from life and business coaching, and yes, I have still never gone to university.

Having now regaled you with a little story and trip down memory lane, I'm delighted to be writing the foreword for this book, the *Coaches Marketing Roadmap*.

When I first started coaching, there was very little knowledge out there about how to become a life coach. Today, there are dozens of highly respected life coaching schools and academies, all across the world, that teach you the skills to be a life coach.

As a result, every year tens of thousands of people graduate from these schools. But unfortunately, many of them struggle to attract new clients and grow their businesses. The reason is that, like with all professions, there's a big difference between being good at the thing and being good at marketing, promoting, selling, and scaling the thing.

That's why I'm delighted to introduce you to my good friend, Cathy Smith, who has written this marvellous book to show people how to grow their life coaching business and make it a wild success.

Over the following pages, you will learn hundreds of invaluable hints and tips from someone who has been there and done that. You will learn how to nail your niche, how to position yourself to grab people's attention, how to attract clients who value what you do and how to get five-star reviews. Then how to scale your business and potentially make hundreds of thousands or even millions of dollars from your coaching business.

Before you dive in, a quick note to share one crucial message: they say that only 10% of people who start a book will actually finish it. Herein lies the difference between failure and success. Kudos to you for starting your journey.

Now that you have embarked on this path, I not only encourage but strongly urge you to make a commitment to yourself. Once you have started, don't stop. Keep going, keep reading until you have reached the last page. This commitment is the line between those who start and those who finish—a distinction between failure and success. While anyone can begin, only a select few persist to the end.

So, keep this book close, an ever-present companion. Pledge to read as much as you can each day. Before you know it, this invaluable book will become a part of you, offering insights that will resonate for the rest of your life. Through this journey, you will make a profound impact on the world, helping not just yourself but potentially hundreds, thousands, or even millions of others along the way.

Dream Big,

Dale Beaumont
Founder & CEO of Business Blueprint®

Introduction

Welcome to the *Coaches Marketing Roadmap*, your comprehensive guide to turning your coaching passion into a thriving business. If you are reading this, chances are you are an incredible coach with a wealth of skills and the enthusiasm to make a real difference. But as many talented coaches discover, passion and skills alone don't guarantee business success. That is where this roadmap comes in.

From defining your unique coaching niche to mastering the art of client conversion, this roadmap walks you through every aspect of running a profitable coaching business. We will begin by exploring how to pinpoint your target audience and then dive into building a compelling brand identity that resonates with your ideal clients. A brand is not just a logo or tagline; it is an experience, one that you will learn to consistently deliver through your coaching programs.

The financial side of a business can often seem daunting, especially when it comes to pricing your valuable services. Fear not: we tackle that too, demystifying the art of pricing and providing you with various models to choose from. You will learn how to lay the groundwork for reaching your ideal audience, develop robust marketing strategies, and understand the channels that resonate with your market.

Sales can be an intimidating aspect of any business since it is the engine that keeps your coaching practice running. This book gives you the tools to navigate sales conversations, turn those initial nos into resounding yeses. We round out the journey by discussing essential self-management skills. After all, your business's success hinges on how well you manage your most important asset—YOU!

Each chapter of this roadmap is designed to equip you with the knowledge, strategies, and confidence you need to create and grow your coaching business.

As you venture through this roadmap, you will find that learning is only part of the equation. To truly make progress, you need to take action. That is why I have included practical activities at the end of each chapter. These are designed to help you implement what you have learned, so don't skip them. Implementation is the real key to transitioning from a passionate coach to a successful coaching business owner.

Buckle up and enjoy the ride. Your roadmap to a thriving coaching practice starts now!

Chapter 1

How to Stand Out on the Coaching Map

In a world increasingly smitten with the transformative power of coaching, standing out may feel like an impossible challenge. You have your certificate, your passion, and your toolkit full of coaching methods, and you are ready to start your business. Guess what, so do hundreds, if not thousands, of other equally passionate, certified coaches. In this crowded landscape, how do you distinguish yourself?

The answer lies in identifying and unlocking your niche.

Defining Your Niche

As a coach, defining your niche is an essential step in building a successful coaching practice.

While it may be tempting to market yourself as a generalist coach who can help with a wide range of issues, defining a niche can be more effective.

When someone hears that you are a coach, the next logical question is often, "What kind of coach?"

Identifying your niche not only answers this question, but it also helps you identify your ideal clients and target your marketing efforts. It allows you to become an expert in a particular area and develop a deep understanding of the challenges and opportunities within that space. This expertise can help you differentiate yourself from other coaches and become known as an authority in your field. You will then stand out and attract clients who are specifically seeking help with the issues you specialise in.

Having a niche helps you to focus on where to go for your continued education and aids in word-of-mouth referrals. Defining your niche also allows you to tailor your coaching approach to meet the unique needs of your clients, which can lead to better outcomes and increased client satisfaction.

You cannot market effectively without a clear understanding of whom you are targeting. Your coaching services will not appeal to everyone, and that is okay. Identify your ideal client by considering factors like age, occupation, challenges they face, and goals they aspire to reach. Tailor your marketing messages to address the specific needs and desires of this group. Without a niche your marketing will be wishy-washy and unappealing.

Exploring Potential Niches

There are so many directions you can take when it comes to choosing a niche. From life coaching aimed at young professionals to relationship coaching for couples to weight loss for busy fathers to leadership for executives wanting to change jobs, and the list goes on. Coaching niche areas include health and wellness, business coaching, career development, entrepreneurship, personal finance, and lots of others.

As a coach, you do not have to have the skills or experience in a particular area to coach. However, building trust as a business coach who has never owned or run a business may be difficult. Often it is not about your actual skills; it is more about your perceived abilities.

Your niche should not only be something that interests you but also something where you can leverage your existing skills and knowledge. You could be passionate about nutrition, but if you have no background or expertise in it, you might struggle to coach people effectively in that field.

Matching Skills and Interests

Your niche should ideally be at the intersection of your skills, your life experiences, your passions, and market demand.

Begin by identifying your strengths and passions. You probably have a broad range of skills, but there will be a few areas where you excel. Take the time to evaluate your experiences, skills, and knowledge base to pinpoint where you can make the most impact. This is also an excellent time to survey former clients or consult mentors to gain an outside perspective on your strengths.

What strengths do you have and what are you passionate about?

- Are you passionate about helping corporate teams improve their dynamics?
- Mid-career women who are struggling with burnout?
- Helping startup founders overcome their business challenges?
- Or do you love aiding individuals in their personal development journey?

Use these examples as inspiration and think about the people who could most benefit from your skill set and your passion.

Example:

My first niche was "Empowering Women in Transition to Choose – What Is Next!"

Cathy Smith Coaching supports middle-aged women to decide what they want to do when they grow up!

I got great results for my clients. It was an intersection between my skill set and where I was at the time. However, it wasn't a space that I wanted to play in forever. My passion has been in marketing for a long time, and although I thought I wanted to do something else for a while, the universe had other ideas. The universe kept sending me new, qualified coaches who were struggling to build their businesses and were beginning to think that this "coaching stuff" wasn't for them. Of course, what could I do but pivot back to marketing?

Market Demand for Your Niche

After assessing your skills and passions, you need to do the market research to see if there is a demand for what you are planning to offer. It is not enough to pick a niche you are passionate about; you also need to determine if people are wanting services in this niche and are they willing to pay for it.

Are people looking for the specific coaching service you plan to offer?

Conduct basic market research using tools and resources like Google Trends, online surveys, social media polls, and competitor analysis. You don't want to enter a niche that's too crowded without being able to stand out, nor do you want to choose a niche so narrow that demand is very limited. Look to see if you can identify the big players in your proposed niche.

Once you have identified a potential niche, test it out before going all in. Offer free coaching sessions, webinars, or workshops targeted at your ideal client. Gather feedback to refine your approach and service offering. Ensure that you are hitting the mark with the type of coaching your niche is looking for. Remember to test and measure.

Identifying Your Target Audience

After assessing the market demand for your niche, you will have a better idea of your target audience.

Who exactly is your target market?

Go beyond demographic details. Understand their pain points, what keeps them up at night, and how you, specifically, can help solve their problems. The more precisely you can define your target audience, the more focused and effective your marketing efforts will be.

Identifying Your Unique Selling Proposition (USP)

To stand out in your niche, you need to understand your Unique Selling Proposition (USP). For some coaches, you might like to think of your USP more as a UVP, a Unique Value Proposition. Selling is something that you will need to do to have a thriving business, but for now, adding value may sit better with you.

What sets you apart from other coaches?

Maybe it is your background in a specific industry or a unique methodology you have developed or adopted. It could even be your personal story that makes you an ideal coach for a particular audience. Take time to recognise what makes you unique and how that uniqueness can fill a gap in the coaching market.

USP or UVP is a clear statement that describes the benefit of your offer, how you solve your customers' needs and add value and what distinguishes you from your competition.

Course Correction

Don't panic if, after a while, you feel like you have picked the wrong niche. Choosing a niche doesn't have to be a one-off decision. As you grow in your career and as market demands change, you may need to review and possibly adapt your niche. Pivoting is a part of business, and the experience you have gained will not go to waste. Learning how to adapt is a crucial skill you will need as a coach and a business owner.

In the end, choosing a niche is about finding the sweet spot between your skills, your passion, and the market demand. By defining what you do, you will also define who you are in the coaching industry.

Unlocking your niche is the crucial first step in standing out in the coaching landscape. It directs your marketing efforts, focuses your services, and helps you create more tailored, effective coaching programs. Most importantly, it ensures that you are offering something truly unique, making it easier to attract and retain the clients who will most benefit from your services. This clarity will make everything from marketing to conducting the actual coaching sessions more focused and effective.

Choose your niche. Just do it. You need to decide on one niche and then go for it. Remember you can change your niche; it is not set in stone. However, swapping and changing niches can be expensive and time-consuming and rarely benefits anyone. Make your choice and go all in for at least 6 months and then re-assess.

Why I Niched

As an artist's granddaughter, I wanted to follow in my grandfather's footsteps. I spent hours in his studio, drawing, playing with clay and watching him work. My grandfather was a sculptor who loved realism in art. He spent hours and hours studying muscle form so that the muscles he created in his drawings and sculptures were lifelike. The muscles on a running horse looked like they were rippling, with the rider's hair flowing in the wind; you could almost feel them rushing past. He niched into lifelike people and animals that made you feel like they were with you, so much so that in later years, he made memorial plaques for cemeteries and crematoriums when he was no longer able to do big pieces. By niching, my grandfather had a 65-year art career that supported his passion, his family, and his life.

Design has been my whole life, although not as an artist. Ultimately, marketing became the way I would channel my creativity. Niching to help coaches like you create a thriving business. It is how I stand out on the crowded marketing map and why you are reading this book now.

> *"The* miracle *is not that I finished.*
> *The miracle is that I had the* courage *to start."*
> *John Bingham*

Activity, Should You Choose to Accept!

The following questions can help you narrow down your niche and develop a focused coaching practice.

1. **Think about these questions when trying to define your niche:**
   What inspires me to wake up every day?

   Why did I become a coach?

   What experiences, skills, qualifications and training do I bring to coaching?

   What parts of my history, previous job, skill set and life experience do I want to leverage with my coaching?

2. **Download the Niche Identification Worksheet.**
   Go to cathysmith.com.au/book-resources and download the Niche Identification Worksheet. List the areas you are interested in and score them 1-10, with 10 being the highest, based on market demand, your expertise, your experience and your passion. The one with the highest score is a strong contender for your niche, see the worksheet for the full instructions.

3. **Client Avatar Worksheet:**
   Also go to cathysmith.com.au/book-resources, download the Client Avatar Worksheet and get the clear on your ideal client.

We Sell Hot Water

In a bustling café nestled in the heart of Melbourne, the aromatic fusion of drinks being prepared was a testament to the diversity of its patrons' choices. As people queued, waiting for their morning pick-me-up, conversations about hot drinks filled the air. Yet, as any connoisseur knows, the realm of hot beverages is vast and varied.

Asking for "a hot drink" in a café is like walking into an expansive library and asking for "a book". As conversations progress, distinctions emerge, leading to that age-old debate: "Are you a coffee person or a tea person?"

In this particular café, coffee enthusiasts were aplenty. Discussions about the origins of beans, the intricacies of brewing methods, and the ideal frothiness of lattes were commonplace. They revelled in the richness of their favourite brew and the complexities that came with it. Yet, amongst these aficionados was Amelia, whose beverage preferences stood in stark contrast.

Amelia's heart belonged to tea. Every facet of tea making, from selecting the leaves to the brewing time, held significance for her. And when she ordered, her requirements were clear: "A pot of Earl Grey for 1, please. And could you keep the milk on the side? Don't put the little caddy inside the cup."

Amelia's pet hate was when milk caddies, which had been sitting on the bench or who knows where else, were placed inside the cup. They would not do that for a coffee drinker, she thought with a sigh.

Now, one might wonder, why not just adapt the language of coffee culture to accommodate Amelia's love for tea?

The answer is simple: it wouldn't resonate.

Asking Amelia about espresso shots or the perfect crema would be incongruent. It is like using the words of a baker to communicate with a potter. The tools, the processes, and the end results differ vastly.

Generalist

At our café, simplicity meets elegance; come savour the pure essence of water, served with precision and care in our beautifully crafted cups. Experience the charm of minimalism, where every sip is a reminder of life's simple pleasures.

Niching

Discover the authentic essence of tea at our teahouse, where each cup transports you on a journey to its pristine origins. Step into a haven of tranquillity and taste, with a curated selection that is sure to tantalise your senses. Embrace the art of tea drinking with us, as every sip becomes an adventure, steeped in tradition and rich flavour.

Which do you think Amelia would be attracted to?

This whole café story is a bit like coaching.

When you are setting up shop as a coach, you need to figure out who you are really chatting to. Like how Amelia is all about her tea, some people need a particular kind of coaching. It is all about finding your groove and understanding your tribe. Just like you wouldn't talk about espresso shots with a tea lover, when you nail down your niche in coaching, you are speaking directly to the hearts of your ideal clients. It is not just about throwing words out there; it is about truly connecting. After all, while general coaching might help, finding that perfect fit between you and your clients—that is a game changer.

When you are casting a super wide net in coaching without narrowing down your niche, your marketing messages just will not hit the mark. When you truly know your clients, get who they are and what they are about, then marketing becomes a whole lot easier, and you will have people lining up to work with you.

The next step, now that you have found your niche, is to build your identity as a coach. This will be the cornerstone of your marketing, your way forward and the focus of our next chapter.

Chapter 2

Crafting an Identity Beyond the Certificate

Once you have decided on your niche, the next task is to think about your brand. A brand that not only serves your clients effectively but will also set you apart in the marketplace. Your brand will be the basis for everything you do moving forward.

How Do You See Yourself as a Coach?

The first step in building a strong brand and a thriving business is self-awareness. You need to know who you are as a coach, what your strengths and weaknesses are, and how you want to be perceived by your potential clients. Take some time to think about your coaching philosophy, your methods and the kind of relationship you want to build with your clients.

Here are 3 questions to think about:

- What are your core values as a coach?
- What are your unique coaching techniques?
- How do you want to make your clients feel?

Having a firm grasp on these elements will set up the foundation for a strong brand identity. A strong brand is not just about a logo and catchphrase; it is about building a coaching practice that reflects who you are.

- How do you see yourself as a coach?
- Are you telling people you are a coach?

If not, that is your first hurdle.

How can someone else believe that you are the right coach for them if you don't believe it yourself?

Build Your Brand: Crafting an Identity Beyond the Certificate

To build a thriving coaching business you need to have a strong brand that your clients can identify with. Think of all the great coaches you know. They all have strong personal and business brands that you can identify with and quickly know what they do and how they help "their people".

Don't be fooled by trying to copy what the big names are doing. They have spent many years and often large sums of money getting to where they are now. Without their years of experience, copying what they are doing will not only be very frustrating for you, but it will simply not work at the level you are now. Often these big coaches get criticised for not following their own advice. This is because different advice, strategies and tactics work at different levels.

Don't judge your chapter 1 on someone else's chapter 20 and beyond.

The Components of Brand Identity

Branding is not just about a catchy logo or a trendy colour scheme. While those are an essential aspect of your brand, your brand identity will comprise several elements, including the following:

- **Visual Elements:** These are the visual cues like your logo, colours and typography that make your brand recognisable.

- **Tone and Voice:** How do you communicate? Is your tone casual or formal? This aspect is vital in crafting your marketing materials and interacting with clients.

- **Customer Experience:** From initial consultation to concluding a coaching session, how smooth and valuable is the journey for your clients?

By understanding and investing time in these components, you will create a cohesive brand identity that speaks volumes before you even say a word.

Creating a Compelling Brand Message

A strong brand message is one that resonates with your target audience. This message should align with your values, your coaching philosophy, and the needs or aspirations of your potential clients.

- **Unique Selling Proposition (USP):** This is the cornerstone of your brand, encapsulating what sets your coaching service apart from others in the most unique way. It is the first thing people should know that differentiates you from competitors.

- **Unique Value Proposition (UVP):** What makes you different from other coaches? It could be your unique methodology or specific expertise in an area. Make sure your value proposition is clear and compelling.

- **Tagline:** This is an optional but impactful element. A catchy tagline can stick in people's minds and effectively summarise your brand message.

You have got this, take one step at a time. Let's start with your USP.

USP - Unique Selling Proposition

A Unique Selling Proposition—USP, is a statement that communicates why a client should choose you over others available in the market. Your USP emphasises the unique benefits, advantages or solutions that your coaching services provide, addressing the specific needs or desires of your target audience.

You may be a newly accredited coach; however, you still have a wealth of knowledge and a raft of expertise. You have lived experiences to draw on.

There are many ways to articulate your USP. Here is a great example to use.

As a coach, you need to identify your unique selling proposition, your USP. You need to articulate your expertise, the benefits of your services or proposed services and why you are different.

Think about these 3 areas to help you identify your USP:

Expertise

1. Understand your unique value: Reflect on your strengths, skills and experiences as a coach. Consider what sets you apart from other coaches. Are you particularly skilled in a specific coaching technique or methodology? Do you have a specialised background or expertise that gives you an edge? Identify the unique qualities that make you stand out.

Benefits

2. Identify the specific benefits: Analyse the needs, desires, and pain points of your target audience. What do they want to achieve through your coaching? How can your expertise and approach help them overcome challenges and achieve their goals? Identify the specific benefits that clients can expect by working with you.

Difference

3. Differentiate yourself by emphasising what you do differently. By combining value and benefits, you bring together the unique value you offer as a coach.

Try this formula.

[AUDIENCE] achieve [TRANSFORMATION] with [SERVICE] and [OUTCOME].

Example

As a marketing coach with over 22 years of experience, my expertise is focused on helping individuals grow their businesses. I empower coaches to uncover their true passions and then teach them how to transform their passion into a successful business. Leveraging my deep knowledge of marketing and personalised coaching techniques, I offer tailored guidance to help my clients identify their message, overcome obstacles, and ultimately create a thriving business.

Remember, your USP should reflect you authentically as a coach and clearly communicate the unique value and benefits you bring to your clients. It should capture their attention, differentiate you from competitors, and make it evident why they should choose you as their coach.

Are you struggling with the idea of creating a USP for yourself?

Many coaches find crafting a USP hard as they don't want to "sell" anyone. What if you shift from a "selling" mindset to a "value-added" mindset?

Unique Value Proposition (UVP) is an alternative to a USP. A UVP could make a world of difference for you, especially if you are not yet comfortable with the concept of selling.

UVP - Unique Value Proposition

A UVP is very similar to a USP, with a few small subtleties. A UVP is essentially your unique identifier in the coaching industry. The unique mix of services, experience and approaches makes you stand out from others in your niche. What you offer adds specific value to your clients' lives. Your UVP is very effective in attracting the right clients and plays a key role in retaining them.

Crafting Your UVP

Here are some steps to help you identify your UVP:

1. **Know Your Audience:** Start by understanding who your target clients are. What problems are they trying to solve? What are their pain points? The better you know them, the easier it will be to tailor your services to meet their needs.

2. **Analyse Competitors:** Look at other coaches in your niche and identify what makes you different. Do you offer a unique methodology? Do you have a particular expertise? Perhaps your coaching style is exceptionally supportive or goal-oriented?

3. **Identify Value:** Once you have gathered this information, think about what value you can add that others can't. It could be something as simple as offering follow-up accountability checks or providing additional resources like e-books and worksheets.

4. **Keep It Simple:** Your UVP should be straightforward. It should communicate clearly what you do, for whom, and how it benefits them.

5. **Test and Measure:** Finally, don't hesitate to test out your UVP and adjust as necessary. As you gain more experience

and feedback, you will get a better understanding of what truly sets you apart.

Your UVP needs to focus on your clients' pain points. By adopting this approach, you will enable them to clearly see the tangible results that they can achieve through your solution.

Try this formula.

[Service] helps [customer] [solve problem] by/through [unique benefit].

Example

Cathy Smith Coaching helps aspiring coaches grow successful businesses by leveraging over 22 years of marketing expertise to empower them in uncovering their true passions, identifying their unique messages, and overcoming obstacles through personalised, tailored guidance.

USP - Unique Selling Proposition and/or UVP - Unique Value Proposition

As you can see, UVPs are only subtly different to USPs. However, removing the word "selling" often helps coaches to articulate their value more easily.

Do you need both a USP and UVP? No. Generally, businesses only choose one. As a coach, choose the proposition that suits you and your clients best.

Creating a Tagline

This is an optional but impactful element. A tagline can also be used as part of your elevator pitch.

What do you do?

Example

I help coaches turn their passion into a thriving business.

A catchy tagline can be easy to remember and tends to stick in people's minds. A good tagline should effectively summarise your brand message. When formulating a tagline, here are some things to consider:

1. **Keep It Short and Simple:** A tagline should be easy to remember, which generally means keeping it under 10 words. Aim to be brief while still being informative.

2. **Reflect Your Brand Identity:** The tagline should encapsulate your Unique Selling Proposition or Unique Value Proposition. It should be in harmony with the overall philosophy of your brand.

3. **Use Clear Language:** Avoid jargon or overly complex words. The goal is to make the tagline immediately understandable and memorable to as broad an audience as possible.

4. **Convey a Benefit:** Your tagline should quickly communicate what a client will gain from working with you. Are you focused on life transformations? Speedy results? Tailored coaching plans? Make that clear.

5. **Test It Out:** Before finalising your tagline, share it with some trusted peers and potential clients to get their feedback. Does it resonate? Is it memorable?

6. **Be Consistent:** Once you have chosen a tagline, use it consistently across all your branding materials and platforms to solidify your brand identity.

Creating a compelling tagline takes time and may require several iterations. Don't rush the process. A strong tagline could be the final touch that brings your brand message together.

Your Elevator Pitch

Having an elevator pitch is a highly beneficial asset for any coach—or business owner, for that matter. While your tagline or slogan serves to quickly encapsulate your brand message, an elevator pitch goes a bit deeper, offering a succinct but comprehensive overview of what you do, who you do it for and why someone should choose to work with you.

Here is why an elevator pitch is useful:

1. **Immediate Clarity:** When someone asks, "What do you do?" an elevator pitch allows you to answer clearly and succinctly without stumbling over your words or offering too vague a response.

2. **Networking:** Whether you are at a business event or a casual gathering, you never know when you will meet a potential client or collaborator. Having an elevator pitch ready ensures you make the most of these serendipitous opportunities.

3. **Focus:** Preparing an elevator pitch forces you to clarify your own thinking about your coaching business. What is its essence? What is most important? These are questions you will need to answer, which will help in other areas of your business as well.

4. **Engagement:** A well-crafted elevator pitch can capture someone's attention and make them want to know more. That opens the door to longer conversations, meetings, and—ultimately—business relationships.

5. **Sales and Marketing:** Your elevator pitch can serve as the backbone for other marketing materials, like your website copy, social media bios and even the introductory section of your business plan.

How to Create an Elevator Pitch:

1. **Start with Who You Are:** Begin by introducing yourself and your role. "I'm a life coach" could be the start, but aim to be more specific, based on your niche.

2. **Identify the Problem You Solve:** Every business exists to solve a problem. State this problem clearly. For example, "I help young professionals suffering from burnout."

3. **Explain Your Solution:** How do you solve this problem? Be concise but informative. "I offer a 12-week holistic program that tackles burnout from all angles."

4. **Why You?** Briefly touch on what makes you unique or qualified. This is where your Unique Selling Proposition might come into play. "With a background in both psychology and corporate management, I bring a unique perspective to combating burnout."

5. **Call to Action:** Conclude by suggesting the next step. "If you are tired of feeling constantly drained, I'd love to chat about how my program could help."

6. **Practice:** An elevator pitch needs to sound natural and conversational, not like you are reading from a script. Practice so you can deliver it smoothly.

Example

I'm a Marketing Coach. I help coaches turn their passion into a thriving business and not just an expensive hobby. The Coaches Marketing Roadmap is a 12-week course that helps newly certified coaches go from overwhelm to their first client and beyond. With 25 years' experience in marketing and business, I can help coaches to create a profitable business doing what they love. If you are not getting traction in your coaching business, give me a call.

Remember, the best elevator pitches are adaptable. You should be able to extend it into a longer conversation if the opportunity arises. Equally, you should be able to truncate it into a single sentence if you are short on time, and that can also double as your tagline.

Don't Get Overwhelmed

As they say, Rome wasn't built in a day, and your identity beyond the certificate won't be either.

The best way to think of it is like an overcoat on a wet, cold day; you can try it on, layer it or remove it completely. Have a bit of fun with your new identity as a coach. Play with your taglines and elevator pitch, see how people react and notice how you feel.

I worked with a client who wanted to coach in rural and regional areas. We created a clear USP and tagline then went on to do the elevator pitch. They all sounded great and clearly articulated them as a coach and the services they offered, but something was just not right. We tossed ideas back and forward for a few weeks, tweaking and changing before finally nailing it. The change we had to make was "rural and regional areas" to "country".

It is often the simple things that make the difference. Don't overcomplicate it. Just do it!

Getting your brand identity right can be a frustrating process for many coaches and will take trial and error, but once you nail it, everything else will fall into place with ease. It is all about how you feel as you say it and whether it lands with your IDEAL client.

Remember, not everyone is your ideal client, and repelling those who aren't isn't a bad thing. More on that later.

> *"A brand is the set of expectations, memories, stories, and relationships that, taken together, account for a consumer's decision to choose one product or service over another."*
> *Seth Godin*

Activity, Should You Choose to Accept!

Here are your exercises for this chapter. Learning is one thing; however, implementing is what really moves the needle.

1. **Decide on a USP or UVP.**
   Which will suit you best?

2. **Now Write it Up.**
   Write your USP - Unique Selling Proposition

   [Audience] achieve [Transformation] with [Service] and [Outcome].

   Or

   UVP - Unique Value Proposition

   [Service] helps [customer] [solve problem] by/through [unique benefit].

3. **Check Out Extra Resources:**
   Go to cathysmith.com.au/book-resources to download more free goodies and extra information to help you craft your identity as a coach. Now that you have started to build your identity as a coach (your brand message), let's extend it into your full brand in the next chapter.

Following the Stars

In the coastal town of Byron Bay, where waves met wisdom, Ella began her journey as a life coach. With her freshly minted certificate in hand, she envisioned her path to be as clear as the sapphire sea. The world of coaching proved to be as unpredictable as the ocean tides.

Amongst the town's vibrant lanes, Ella saw coaches whose names glittered like the stars. Their brands had a magnetic pull, drawing people in with an almost hypnotic allure. Smitten by their success, Ella thought, "If I can recreate their magic, surely I can shine just as brightly."

With starry-eyed ambition, Ella began copying them. She adopted their styles, their words, and their aesthetics. She even hosted seminars, echoing their mantras and methods. Yet, instead of attracting a tidal wave of clients, she found herself adrift in a vast sea, with no compass to guide her.

One evening, as the sun painted the sky with hues of amber and gold, Ella found herself in a quaint café. There, she met Maya, a local coach whose fame hadn't reached the stars but whose impact had deeply touched the community. Maya's brand was woven with threads of her own story, her struggles, her triumphs, and her genuine connection with her clients.

Inspired by Maya's authenticity, Ella had a revelation. She realised she had been trying to navigate using someone else's map. She needed to chart her own course.

With renewed vigour, Ella embarked on a journey of introspection. She delved into her past, her passions, and her purpose. She reshaped her brand, intertwining it with her own narrative, her unique coaching techniques, and the emotions she wanted to evoke.

As the days turned into months, Byron Bay began to whisper tales of the coach with a brand as authentic as the ocean's song. Ella's sessions became sanctuaries of genuine connection. The town didn't just see her as another coach; they saw Ella, with all her depth, passion, and authenticity.

Through her journey, Ella learned that in the vast ocean of coaching, it is not the brightest stars that guide you; it is the coach who really connects with you and understands the problem you need help solving.

When you are trying to wear a brand that doesn't truly fit, your message gets muddled and lost in the crowd. However, when you embrace a brand that resonates with your authentic self, it speaks volumes, even in whispers. It is about being genuine, connecting with your unique story, and sharing it with the world. When your brand is a true reflection of you, it shines brighter and draws clients to you like a beacon. They become eager to experience the authenticity you bring to the table.

The next step for you as a coach, now that you have started to build your identity, your brand message, is to extend it into your full brand in Chapter 3.

Chapter 3

Turning Identity into a Brand

Congratulations, you have done the groundwork for starting your brand.

You have defined your Unique Selling Proposition or Unique Value Proposition; you have crafted an elevator pitch and maybe you even came up with a snazzy tagline.

If not, I suggest you stop right here, go back to Chapter 2 and at least get your ideas down on paper. Do a thought dump of everything that you can think of before moving on to this chapter.

Yes, on paper.

According to a study by the University of Tokyo, writing by hand Increases the brain's ability to recall tasks over taking notes on a tablet or smartphone.

A Well-Designed Logo

A well-designed logo can be a powerful tool in establishing and promoting your brand identity. However, many coaches find themselves stuck at this stage. If the lack of a logo is hindering you from getting started, feel free to skip this section and come back later.

Having a logo that reflects your identity can give you the confidence to get out there and market your coaching business. Yet, there's no need to spend hundreds of dollars perfecting it before engaging with potential clients. Logos often evolve over many months, so just start now.

Here are some key elements to think about for your logo so that it will align with your overall brand strategy.

1. Simplicity and Relevance

Less is often more. A simple logo can be easily recognised and remembered. You don't want to confuse potential clients with overly complex designs. Your logo should reflect your coaching style and area of expertise.

Example

If you are a life coach focusing on stress management, softer colours and smooth lines could better represent your brand rather than sharp, angular shapes.

2. Unique and Adaptable

Your logo needs to set you apart from the competition. Opting for a design that incorporates elements unique to your brand's identity, like a clever play on your initials or a symbol that encapsulates your values, can work well.

Think ahead, as your logo will need to be used in multiple situations, from business cards to your website, social media and potentially signage. Ensure it looks good in various sizes and colour situations, like monochrome, black and white, reverse and colour.

3. Colour Palette

Colours play a significant role in shaping emotions and perceptions, which is why it is crucial to choose a colour scheme that aligns with your brand's values and messaging. Most successful logos only have 1 or 2 colours in them. Think about a primary colour and then combine it with a second colour. Colours have meanings and create emotions within us. Here are some to think about:

- Blue: Often signifies trust, strength, calmness and reliability. It is a popular choice for brands that want to instil a sense of stability and integrity.

- Green: Symbolises growth, renewal and health. This colour is great for coaches focusing on personal development or wellness.

- Red: Conveys passion, excitement and urgency. Consider using red to draw attention and provoke action but use it sparingly to avoid inducing stress.

- Yellow: Represents optimism, cheerfulness and enthusiasm. This bright and attention-grabbing colour can uplift the spirits but can be overwhelming if overused.

- Orange: Combines the energy of red and the happiness of yellow to represent enthusiasm, creativity, confidence and success. It is less intense than red but still commands attention.

- Purple: Associated with luxury, wisdom, imagination and ambition. This colour can lend a touch of sophistication and elegance to your brand.

- Black: Denotes strength, authority and sophistication. It can make other colours stand out, but use it cautiously as it can also evoke strong emotions.

- Grey: Signifies neutrality, balance, calm, authority and sophistication. It is often used in corporate settings and can serve as an excellent background to make other colours stand out. However, it is crucial to pair grey with more vibrant colours to avoid a dull or monotonous look.

- White: Symbolises purity, simplicity and cleanliness. It is often used in branding to create a sense of space and simplicity.

Your brand's colour scheme should not only be visually appealing but should also communicate the right emotions and ideas to your potential clients. Keep these meanings in mind when choosing the primary and secondary colours that will represent your coaching business. Your brand's colour scheme should be consistent with your overall branding strategy.

4. Typography

Fonts matter. Whether it is serif, sans-serif, or script, the typography used in your logo should align with the tone and feel of your brand.

Example

A corporate coaching business might opt for a sleek, modern font, often sans-serif.

A wellness coach might go for something more organic, flowing serif or script font.

Script fonts often look formal and can be hard to read. If you have your heart set on a script font, consider using it for only 1 letter or 1 word as an accent rather than all the text of your logo.

5. Scalable and Cohesive

Ensure that your logo looks crisp and clear whether it is on a business card or a billboard. Vector formats are usually the best for this as they can be scaled up or down in size without distortion.

If you already have established brand elements like a tagline or specific imagery, consider how your logo can incorporate or complement these elements.

6. Memorable and Timelessness

At the end of the day, you want your logo to stick in people's minds. Unique yet appropriate design elements can make your logo memorable, contributing to brand recognition.

Trends come and go, but a great logo can stand the test of time. Aim for a design that you won't have to change every few years because it now looks dated as the trend has passed.

Example

Cathy Smith Coaching Brand

The logo uses the 2 Cs from Cathy and Coaching.

A heart symbol in the middle.

Purple colouring leading into Magenta (Strong Pink), wisdom, imagination and quality.

Magenta also pulls in my past where I started my career in printing. Magenta is the M in CMYK, the 4 offset printing colours, which was the only form of commercial printing back then.

There are many tones in this logo; however, there are only 2 main colours— Purple and Magenta.

The design elements give this logo its complex yet simple elegance.

The logo has also stood the test of time, including when I pivoted my direction back to marketing.

As you can see, the Cathy Smith Coaching logo has covered all the elements for a quality logo with longevity.

Leveraging Your Brand into Tangible Actions

A brand is more than just a few well-chosen words or a cool logo. While these are important elements, there's more to the story. A good brand is an experience that you offer your clients from the moment they hear about you to the end of your coaching relationship and beyond. Your brand acts as a silent ambassador for your services, underpinning every aspect of your coaching business.

Your brand should be evident in every interaction with your client. From the introductory email or call to the consultation, coaching sessions and follow-up, your brand values should shine through. This goes beyond mere aesthetics or taglines; it reaches into the very fabric of how you conduct business.

Example

If one of your brand values is transparency, this should be reflected in straightforward and open communication with your clients. If you emphasise growth and development, your coaching space—whether physical or virtual—should inspire a sense of possibility and evolution.

This consistency across different touchpoints not only helps in building credibility but also fosters a sense of familiarity and trust with your clients. It is about more than just what you say; it is also about how you say it, the tools you use to communicate and even the setting in which your coaching takes place. The goal is to create a seamless and positive experience that aligns perfectly with what your brand stands for. Your branding tells a story, so make sure it is telling the one you want, and make sure that story is integrated throughout your business.

Marketing Your Brand

Marketing your coaching business goes beyond merely selling your services. Marketing is more than the sum of its parts; it is about consistently conveying your brand message to your target audience. The essence of your brand should take centre stage in all your marketing initiatives.

Whether you choose a marketing strategy that involves leveraging the power of word-of-mouth referrals, investing in paid advertising, creating a fabulous website or taking advantage of free social media platforms, what is essential is that your brand's unique essence is at the forefront of all your efforts. We will discuss crafting an effective marketing strategy in more detail in Chapter 6, but for now, let us focus on how your brand plays a pivotal role in your overall marketing approach.

Example

If "empowerment" is a cornerstone of your brand, you might consider offering free mini-coaching sessions or workshops focusing on self-improvement and personal growth. Sharing these through your social media channels or as part of your email marketing campaign allows you to embody the transformative experiences you offer. This not only underlines your brand's core value but also creates an attractive narrative that speaks directly to potential clients who are looking to make meaningful changes in their lives.

Your brand serves as the lens through which people see your business. Your website, every blog post, social media update or advertising campaign should reflect the core values and messages that make your coaching service unique. This ensures a cohesive and trustworthy brand experience for your audience.

Remember, a brand is not set in stone; it evolves just as you and your coaching business do. This is why it is crucial to make time to review your branding efforts periodically. Evaluating your brand is not a one-time event but an ongoing process. You should listen to client feedback, assess your competition and adapt to market changes to ensure you are staying aligned with your business goals and your brand's essence.

This will help you keep your marketing strategies effective and relevant, ensuring you continue to connect with your audience in a meaningful way.

Example

By matching your branding to your clients' expectations, your business can become the only choice. This is what happened to one of my clients recently. John was not getting the traction he needed to make his business grow. His work was great, and his clients loved him, but he just couldn't get enough leads. We worked on his branding and the messaging he was sending out. He always introduced himself as the personal branding expert. When we delved deeper, his clients weren't coming to him for personal branding; they wanted to be influencers. After changing the words, John now has plenty of leads coming to his business every day.

Your brand is more than just a logo or a catchy phrase; it is a promise of value, an assurance of quality and a marker of the unique coaching experience that only you can provide. Leverage it wisely, and you will build a legacy rather than just a business.

> *"Building a brand means knowing your story and building and sharing that story."*
> *Tamara McCleary*

Activity, Should You Choose to Accept!

Phew, breathe. That was a lot to take in. Here are the exercises for this chapter. Remember, understanding is good, but action is what truly brings your brand to life.

1. **Create a Brand Narrative.**
   Write a brief narrative describing the ideal client experience from their first contact with you to the end of a coaching session. Use this as a guide for all client interactions.

2. **Test Your Brand Experience.**
   Enlist a friend to go through the client journey with you. From the first point of contact to consultation and follow-up, ask for feedback on how well your brand values are coming through.

3. **Check Out Extra Resources:**
   For more detailed exercises and tools that can help you in leveraging your brand, head over to cathysmith.com.au/book-resources.

A Cup Full or More

On a sunlit day by a serene lake, young Lucy was enjoying a lakeside holiday with her grandfather when she asked him for some lime cordial.

"Of course," her grandfather replied, handing her a capful of the cordial. "Now, go down to the lake and pour it in there," he instructed.

Lucy found this odd, but knowing her grandfather's generous nature, she thought perhaps she might end up transforming the entire lake into a delicious, lime-flavoured drink. With that hope, she went ahead.

After pouring the capful of lime cordial concentrate into the lake, she scooped up a big cupful to taste. "Yuck!" she exclaimed.

When Lucy drank a mouthful of the drink, she immediately spat it out. It tasted like swamp water straight from the lake.

Her grandfather, seeing her reaction, chuckled heartily. "It tastes so bad!" Lucy exclaimed.

"Why don't you try putting it in a cup with only a little bit of water this time?" suggested her grandfather, pouring some more cordial for her. When she did, the result was a delightful, zesty drink that Lucy thoroughly enjoyed.

"Could you taste the cordial in the lake?" her grandfather queried. Lucy shook her head in response.

"Life is the same," he began. "To get things right, you need more concentration on the task at hand, rather than attempting to flavour an entire lake with just a capful of cordial."

This tale mirrors a crucial concept in business. Does your brand resonate like a potent, memorable cordial in a glass, or does it get lost, diluted in a vast lake of generic messages?

One of my favourite sayings is "Talking to everyone is talking to no one."

If your marketing is too generic, your potential clientele may miss the unique "flavour" you bring. In today's fast-paced world, clear and relatable messaging is not a mere luxury; it is imperative. Ask yourself, is your brand message concentrated and impactful, or is it a diluted afterthought? Remember, for genuine impact, sometimes less truly is more.

These focused steps will serve as a strong foundation for your brand, helping you engage more effectively with your clients. Chapter 4 is about creating a powerful coaching toolbox that will give you the confidence to go out and have conversions with prospective clients.

Chapter 4

Your Powerful Coaching Toolbox

Keep going. Now the fun starts.

You have defined your niche and chosen your brand, and you know exactly who your target audience is. The critical next step is to create a coaching program that meets the unique needs of your clients. This is where the rubber meets the road. Your program will be the product that you are offering, the solution to your clients' problems.

Crafting a coaching program that serves your clients' needs effectively will set you apart in the marketplace and be a huge drawcard for your audience. If you think of your coaching practice as a car, then your programs will be the gears that drive it forward. A well-designed program can be the difference between a fleeting client and a long-term relationship.

Understanding Your Client's Journey

To craft an effective coaching program, it is essential to understand the journey your clients will go on when they choose to work with you. This adds depth to your program and can help you tailor it to meet the individual needs of your clients.

Begin by mapping out the journey you would like to take your clients on.

- Are they coming to you for career development?
- Business coaching?
- Personal growth?

- General life coaching?
- Specific life coaching (e.g. weight loss, relationships, etc.)?

Knowing the starting point allows you to customise your approach for different levels of experience.

In a coaching program, the client journey typically starts with an initial consultation to identify needs and set goals. Customised 1 on 1 sessions then dive into targeted areas for growth. Milestones are set to track progress and adjust strategies. Group sessions may introduce community support and diverse perspectives. Online modules offer flexibility, letting clients refine skills at their own pace. Regular reviews assess achievements and recalibrate goals, culminating in a final evaluation that celebrates the client's progress and maps out future growth. This blended approach ensures a tailored, effective and rewarding coaching experience.

Example
This client testimonial by Graeme Willox.

"The Coaches Marketing Roadmap was right place, right time for me. I had been struggling for a while to find a presence as a coach but definitely found it in the Coaches Marketing Roadmap.

The unique combination of the weekly group discussions that Cathy was able to coach and personalise to our own particular situations, followed by the mentoring of then "How" to market this to our own particular targeted audience has been brilliant.

Through the Coaches Marketing Roadmap I was able to find the clarity, confidence and direction I was looking for in regards to what my coaching stood for and how I could represent and now market that and myself as a coaching business the way I have always wanted and I thoroughly recommend Cathy and her program to anyone looking to do the same."

Many coaches find success by offering a blend of coaching methods, such as a structured program with a combination of 1 on 1 and group calls. This provides a good balance of scalability and personalisation, especially in a corporate setting or when you are ready to grow. The lowest hanging fruit is 1 to 1, so if you are undecided start there and work up.

The most important thing is to ensure that you structure your coaching program in a way that benefits both you and your clients. It should allow you to set achievable goals with your clients and effectively measure their progress.

Types of Coaching for Your Program

You have 4 choices:

- 1 on 1 Coaching
- Group Coaching
- Online Program / Structured Course
- Hybrid Coaching

1 on 1 Coaching

This is the most personalised form of coaching where the focus is solely on 1 client at a time. This close connection allows for deep work and can yield rapid results. However, it also requires a significant time investment from you, limiting the number of clients you can handle simultaneously and therefore restricting growth.

Group Coaching

Group coaching is an excellent way to serve more clients in a single time slot. While it lacks the 1 on 1 focus, the group dynamic can add an extra layer of accountability and community support for your clients. It is an excellent way to add depth to your program while increasing your revenue.

Online Program / Courses

These are often self-guided programs with predetermined modules and resources. Online programs or courses are scalable and allow you to reach an unlimited number of clients without putting in extra hours. However, you need to be aware that they often lack the personalised touch that some clients desire. Online programs often come with group coaching calls to incorporate the contact time that many clients need.

Hybrid Models

In a hybrid model, you can do a combination of online modules with group or 1 on 1 calls. Clients benefit from personalised 1 on 1 sessions for targeted growth while also enjoying the community support and accountability of group sessions. Online modules provide flexibility, allowing them to learn at their own pace or to provide extra learning resources. This blended approach offers a tailored yet scalable solution to meet your diverse client needs. A hybrid model often works well in a corporate setting.

Each coaching type has its advantages and drawbacks, and understanding these will help you choose the best fit for your coaching practice.

STOP

Walk before you run.

How do you eat an elephant?

1 bite at a time.

Choose a small elephant so that you can get a few quick wins. Start with something manageable and get in a few clients before trying to build the Great Wall of China.

Creating a coaching program is about designing a transformational journey. The impact you make through your program will not only help your clients but also strengthen your coaching practice, setting the stage for lasting success.

Example
This client testimonial by David Ucyurek

"Cathy taught me how to think again. To trust my own instincts and to dare to plan a future that I wanted."

Structuring Your Sessions

Now that you know your clients' needs, you can start to consider how to structure your sessions. Tailoring your approach to meet these needs will set the stage for successful outcomes.

Core Framework

Outline the core framework of your coaching sessions. This might include an introductory phase to set the agenda, a main section for coaching and exercises and a closing phase for reflection and planning next steps.

Time Allocation

Discuss how to allocate time effectively within each session. This will help keep sessions focused and ensure that each coaching touchpoint is effective.

Tools and Techniques

Identify the tools and techniques that you have in your toolbox and which ones to incorporate into your sessions. This could range from questioning models like GROW (developed by Sir John Whitmore), or Wheel of Life. Do you have specific exercises tailored to your coaching niche? What tools are in your toolbox?

Remember, less is often more.

Keep it simple and don't overwhelm your clients with lots of different tools or models.

Setting Goals and Measuring Progress

A quick win can be to start with a goal-setting exercise.

Utilise frameworks like SMART Goals (Specific, Measurable, Achievable, Relevant, Time bound) to set goals that are both challenging and attainable. Explain how setting SMART goals can provide clear direction and make it easier to track progress. The goals should be aligned with what the client wishes to achieve through your coaching program, especially if it is a 1 on 1 program. You can check in and revise the goals of your coaching program several times if you are running a multi-month program to make sure everyone is on track.

"Coaching showed me how to own my own dreams, goals and ideas and keep them in check. Cathy's patience and smiles really kept me in check when I was going off course."

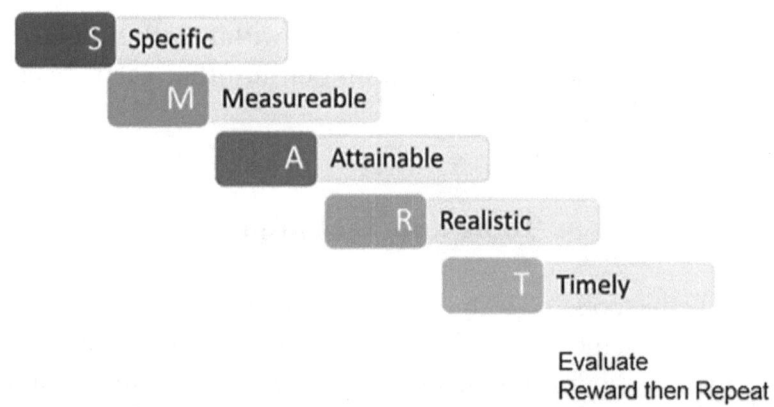

Cathy Smith Coaching

Milestones and Tracking

Depending on your niche and your client's goals, setting milestones and tracking progress can be important. Milestones that align with larger objectives serve as checkpoints, helping to measure the client's progress throughout the coaching program. To track this progress, explore various methods like journals, progress bars or regular check-ins, choosing the one that best fits both your coaching style and your client's needs.

Regular reviews of goals and milestones allow for 1 on 1 program adjustments, keeping everything in tune with the client's evolving needs and circumstances. For online programs, you may consider quizzes or awards to motivate your clients to keep going through the course. By offering a structured approach to session planning and goal setting, you empower your clients to maximise the benefits of your coaching program.

> *"Success is the sum of small efforts, repeated day in.*
> *And day out."*
> *Robert Collier*

Activity, Should You Choose to Accept!

To round off this chapter, remember that your coaching program is more than just a set of sessions. It is the engine that propels your practice forward.

Tailor your programs carefully to meet the unique needs and aspirations of your clients, and you will not only enrich their lives but also ensure a sustainable and thriving business for yourself. So, buckle up and enjoy the rewarding journey ahead.

1. **Your Offering**
   Draft Your First Program. Write what you are going to offer. 1 on 1 or group, how many sessions, what is included? Get a piece of paper out and start brainstorming.

2. **Be Do Have**
   Download the Be Do Have exercise and write down what you need to do to see yourself as a coach, the expert.

3. **Check out Extra Resources:**
   For more detailed exercises and tools that can help you leverage your brand, head over to cathysmith.com.au/book-resources.

Are You Listening?

According to popular legend, Franklin Roosevelt, the 32nd President of the United States, is said to have often felt unheard. Despite his position of power, he believed that people weren't truly listening to him. To test his theory, he devised a little experiment.

During one of his routine receptions at the White House, where he would meet countless individuals, he decided to murmur a shocking sentence to each person in greeting: "I murdered my grandmother this morning."

The responses he received were generic and almost automatic.

"Marvelous!"
"Keep up the good work."
"God bless you, Mr President."

It seemed his suspicions were right; no one was truly listening.

Finally, Roosevelt made it to the end of the receiving line reaching the ambassador from Bolivia. With a discreet lean, the ambassador whispered back, "I'm sure she had it coming."

As a coach, our primary role is to listen. We may have numerous tools and frameworks at our disposal, but they should serve as aids, not crutches. Each client has a unique story, and it is our job to truly hear it. While frameworks provide structure, genuine connection arises from active listening. It is through this connection that we can make a significant difference in our client's journey.

Now you have your first coaching program! You are amazing; well done. Now you have to put a price on it. Yes, if you want this to be a business, clients have to pay you.

Chapter 5

Setting Your Price for Success

One of the most daunting tasks for new coaches, especially those fresh out of certification, is setting their prices. Money can be an awkward topic for many, and when it comes to assigning a monetary value to something as personal as coaching, the task can feel enormous. However, your prices don't just determine your income; they send a message about the value you offer, target a particular clientele and play a pivotal role in the sustainability of your coaching business.

After all, you want this to be a business, not just an expensive hobby, don't you?

Example

Years ago, I was in Devonport, a small town in Tasmania, Australia, walking down the street with a group of people from across the country. We came across a real estate sign on a block of land. 2 people stopped in their tracks.

"Wow, that is so cheap," one said.

The other looked at him oddly and said, "No, way overpriced."

Who was right and who was wrong?

The difference was that the first person was from Sydney, a big capital city where land prices were high. The other was from Hobart, just down the road, where local prices were much cheaper.

Price is about perception.

The Psychology of Pricing

Believe it or not, pricing is just a number. However, it is also deeply tied to psychology. A low price might attract bargain hunters, but it can also deter those who equate higher cost with higher quality. Conversely, a high price might convey premium service but could be unaffordable for a segment of your target market. Striking a balance is key, and that begins with understanding the psychology behind pricing.

Pricing needs to match the customer's perception and how you portray your offering.

McDonald's is never going to be able to charge a premium price. Love them or hate them, you get basically what you pay for, and it is the same in all the stores (with a few cultural differences if you are travelling overseas). McDonald's is not selling premium; it is selling familiarity, consistency and comfort.

The Hilton Hotels, on the other hand, are premium, luxury. Their rooms are soundproofed, your experience is unique, the locations and exclusive perks are amazing, and the list goes on. The Hilton is a premium hotel chain, and you pay for the privilege.

Pricing disconnect can alienate your potential customers.

If you saw a BMW car listed for $30,000, what is your first thought?

Is it old or stolen, or what is wrong with it? Right.

If the same ad was for a 2005 Hyundai Accent, then you would be laughing at the typo. $3,000, not $30,000, and even then, it would have to be in mint condition.

Some people pay a lot of money for a very flashy car, and other people wouldn't even dream of paying that. And it is not necessarily the cost of that car or that some cars are built so much better. It is about how we perceive the car and the way we value it.

Coaching is just the same. There are coaches charging a fortune for coaching with happy clients lining up to pay. Other coaches are coaching for nothing or doing it very, very cheaply.

Calculating Your Worth

When you are thinking about your pricing, think about what you are offering.

Is your process seamless and smooth from consult to onboarding? Do you have an intake video? Are all your emails perfect, the booking system spot on, your branding and website flawless, etc.?

Yes, then you can probably offer a premium price.

Let's face it; if that was you, then you wouldn't be reading this book. You have got it all together, and you are off to the racetrack.

It is okay, don't beat yourself up. You need to start at where you are.

Where do you start when thinking about a number?

Just pick a number, they say. Well, that is not very helpful.

Let us be a bit more constructive than that. Here are some things to think of when navigating the landscape of pricing. Establishing a price that works for you and your client will pave the way for successful business. Remember, not everyone is your ideal client. Your prices will weed out some of these people right away, and that is a good thing.

Your Pricing – Where to Start

The first thing you need to think about is how much money you want or need to make.

Let's say $100,000 for nice round figures. You can decide whether that is for a year, month or day. Don't laugh; some very successful coaches do make that in a day. Brooke Castillo made $52 million in 2023. She also started 20 years ago. This might not be something you aspire to, but you need to start making money if you want a thriving business.

How Many People Do You Need?

1 program at	$100,000
2 programs at	$50,000
4 programs at	$25,000
10 programs at	$10,000
20 programs at	$5,000
100 programs at	$1,000
1,000 programs at	$100

The more you charge, the fewer people or programs you will need to sell to make your $100,000. Price is more about value than the actual number. If your clients think that they will get more value than the dollars they are paying, then the buying decision will be a "Heck Yes!"

The price you should charge is about the value you are giving them. It is the confidence you have when you say the price. If that price makes you feel icky, then it is also going to make your clients feel icky. Price is always what you perceive your value is and the value that you are showing to others. And sometimes it is not even about you.

What you can charge or should charge is more about your clients and your potential clients. You may not think that you would pay that amount for coaching, and you probably wouldn't. That doesn't mean that you can't charge it because it is about them, not about you. It is about what you are offering, who you are offering it to and how you are offering it. If your price is a good value proposition, then people will happily pay it. Not all people but your people.

Your Value

Your price should reflect your worth, so don't underestimate the unique value you bring to your coaching relationships. Factor in your qualifications, experience, unique coaching methodologies and any special skills or resources that enhance your coaching service.

If you are thinking that you don't have any experience, think again. Your life is filled with valuable experiences from everything you have navigated so far to reach this point. Your past experiences, even if they were in a different field, contribute to the unique qualities that define you.

Competitor Research, or Not

What your competitors are charging, frankly, is none of your business.

Investigating the pricing strategies of other coaches in your niche is, in my opinion, a waste of your time. You don't know what went into their pricing decisions and why. Stay in your lane and run your own race.

Competitor research will not tell you what the market can bear or help you position yourself competitively. It will just put ideas in your head that will not be helpful.

- I am too cheap.
- I couldn't charge that.
- No one will pay that.
- I am worth so much more.

Your rates should reflect your unique value proposition, not just be a reaction to someone else's pricing.

Allow People to Buy

No one likes to be sold to by the sleazy car salesman.

When we have a problem, we do like to buy a simple, cost-effective solution that suits our needs without a lot of drama.

Give your clients an easy way to buy.

Offering multiple coaching packages at different price points allows your clients to choose the program that suits them best. Don't assume; allow your people to make their own choices. Make it easy for them to buy with contracts and credit card facilities all set up so you don't have to go back and chase payments later.

Empowering your clients in their buying decisions is a fabulous way to start your coaching relationship.

Example

I was on a consult with a potential client, and we had established that we were a good fit. By offering 1 on 1 coaching or a group program, I allowed the client to make up their own mind and happily see the value in the 1 on 1 coaching package that at first glance they had thought was a bit expensive.

Discounting is a race to the bottom, and selling from a place of scarcity is never a good feeling for anyone.

Don't decrease your price unless you really need to, and be prepared to raise it quickly once you get a few clients. No one likes to find out that new people are being charged less than they are. The gym industry does this very badly, always offering new customers better rates than loyal existing customers. It leaves a bad taste and will often cause people to change gyms. Don't treat your coaching clients in the same way.

Did you know that the beauty industry often thrives when the economy takes a downturn? People who would normally go on holidays are not able to afford it when things are tougher, so they book a little pampering instead.

Coaches created a lot of value and made a lot of money in the COVID-19 pandemic, so don't think you have to cut your rates if the economy dips or market conditions are hard. All you need to do is show that your coaching services are even more valuable at times like these.

Remember, not everyone is your client.

You can always have a low-tier offering like a book or a free podcast for those people who are not seeing the value you are offering just yet.

Your Prices Don't Have to Be Set in Stone

Don't be afraid to adjust your pricing up as you go. You might start with an introductory rate to attract initial clients and then reassess your pricing base as your demand increases. Once you get a few clients under your belt and some results, you will be more comfortable to increase your pricing level. You might even find clients suggesting that you do.

Increasing your pricing is a must to create a thriving business. Communicate changes clearly, give existing clients plenty of notice, and you could grandfather long term clients in at their existing rate for a set period.

Be transparent about your rates and what each package includes. Hidden fees can ruin client relationships. Also, consider offering payment plans. Some clients may be willing to commit to a longer-term coaching relationship if they can spread out the costs.

Your pricing is far more than just slapping a monetary value on your services; it is an intricate dance involving psychology, market conditions, your own worth and a host of other factors. With careful planning and a willingness to adapt, you can set prices that not only cover your costs but also reflect your value, attract the right clients and contribute to your long-term success as a coach.

Money Dramas

If you are experiencing money dramas and are worried about charging too much or making money when you think your services should be free, think about all the good things that you could do if you had more money.

Doing good in the world costs money, so why not make more money and amplify the good that you can do?

Handling Pricing Objections

Pricing objections are a common challenge for coaches and can be a great opportunity to demonstrate the value you bring to the table. When a potential client is hesitant about the cost, it is crucial to shift the focus from price to value. Highlight the transformational benefits they will gain; show them the unique expertise you offer and compare where they are now and the long-term value of their new results. Offering flexible payment plans or tiered pricing options can also ease concerns. Show the client that the proposed price is an investment in their own growth and success, rather than a mere expense.

Addressing common objections in your marketing can make clients feel more comfortable before they even speak to you, significantly reducing the number of objections you will need to handle. We will discuss this more in Chapter 10, "Turning 'A No' Into 'Yes' for Client Success".

Price Is Just a Number

The price you set for your services is just a number, and you can change it.

Set a price, go out to the market, see how it feels, see if you have got the confidence to say that PRICE. It is a good thing to have it just a little bit higher than what you think it should be, but have the confidence to say that price.

> *"Price is what you pay. Value is what you get."*
> *Warren Buffett*

Activity, Should You Choose to Accept!

Setting the right price is a strategic move. It is a declaration of the value you bring to the table and a critical factor in turning your coaching passion into a sustainable, profitable business. So, get comfortable with your numbers; they are the ticket to your long-term success.

1. **Calculate Your Expenses**
   List all your expenses and calculate how much you need to earn.

2. **Set Your Price.**
   Do the pricing exercise earlier in this chapter.

   - How many clients do you need?
   - What do you need to charge?
   - Is that a good price?
   - Set a price and try it out.

3. **Check out Extra Resources:**
   For more detailed exercises and tools that can help you in leveraging your brand, head over to cathysmith.com.au/book-resources.

An Undervalued Price Does Not Benefit Anyone

In the heart of Victoria, nestled between historical landmarks and bustling market streets, lay a quaint artist's nook. It belonged to Claire, a brilliant artisan renowned for her hand-painted porcelain dishes. The sunlit shop was a treasure trove, filled with dishes that told tales through intricate designs and personal touches. Each piece was a testament to Claire's dedication and passion, woven into porcelain through strokes of vibrant colours.

However, as a newcomer to Victoria's vibrant art scene, Claire's confidence in her own craft was still building. Her pricing reflected this apprehension. She hoped that by keeping her prices accessible, she would entice more patrons to take home a piece of her art. The genuine value of her work was, without a doubt, far more than the modest price tags suggested. Claire's heart always raced with anxiety at the mere thought of raising her prices, fearing she'd drive away her cherished customers.

One day, her shop's bell chimed, signalling the arrival of a visitor. Martin, with eyes that sparkled with years of art appreciation, stepped in. As he wandered through the shop, he paused often, losing himself in the stories each dish narrated. What truly astonished him, though, were the prices. They seemed incongruent with the exceptional quality of Claire's work.

Martin struck up a conversation with Claire. Intrigued and sensing Claire's underestimation of her own talent, Martin shared a story. He related a tale of a famed European artist whose paintings were initially overlooked, not because of their quality but because of their surprisingly low prices. People assumed that the low price tag meant the paintings were of mediocre value. However, when the artist boldly raised his prices, not only did sales soar, but art lovers also began to truly appreciate the depth and worth of his work.

Martin's words were a mirror reflecting Claire's own journey and potential. Empowered, Claire re-examined her work's true worth, accounting for the countless hours, the depth of passion, and the unmatched skill. Inspired by Martin's story, Claire decided to take a leap of faith. She re-evaluated the hours, passion, and skill that went into each dish and set her prices accordingly.

While some locals were initially taken aback by the increase, most of them had bought a piece or 2 before the price rise just to support Claire. Now they knew the bargain that they had and began to view her dishes with a newfound respect. They had unknowingly acquired masterpieces at a fraction of their true value.

Word travelled fast. The tale of the talented Australian artist selling invaluable art for a song morphed into stories of a maestro whose pieces were priceless heirlooms. As art enthusiasts from various corners of the country began pouring into her shop, Claire's once quiet nook buzzed with admiration and recognition. In redefining her prices, Claire had not just elevated her income; she had transformed her legacy, cementing her status as one of Australia's premium artists.

This story underscores a pivotal business principle. Price isn't just a number; it is a reflection of perceived value. While setting a price, coaches, like artists, need to consider the depth, expertise, and unique value they bring to the table. It is about more than what clients will pay; it is also about making them understand the transformative journey they are investing in. A well-set price can change one's income and the trajectory of their business story for years to come.

You have achieved so much so far. Congratulations.

Or, whoops, you have not been doing the work. May be time to stop and go back and do the work before moving on to the next step: preparing to attract your ideal audience.

Chapter 6

Laying the Groundwork to Attract Your Ideal Audience

Your coaching expertise is just one stop on the roadmap to building a thriving coaching business. The next critical destination is getting your marketing strategy spot on. Effective marketing can put you in front of potential clients who have the pain points that your solution solves.

The magic to finding clients who love you is to identify your ideal audience and speak their language. You must get inside their heads and know their thoughts.

Have you had that experience from the other side?

You have read the ad or watched the video:

- Nodding, yes, that is me.
- Yes, that is my problem.
- Yes, I do that.
- Yes, I want that.
- Yes, I don't want that to happen anymore.
- Yes, yes, yes.

That is what you need to do for your clients.

Marketing 101, and then you are done. You will have a line of prospects a mile long.

Like everything, it is not that easy, especially when your clients often cannot articulate, even to themselves, what their problem is.

You have laid the groundwork with your qualifications, pricing strategy and brand identity, and now it is time to get some fabulous clients who love you. No matter how skilled you are as a coach, without clients, you don't have a business. This is a crucial chapter because many businesses fail as they don't understand the importance of a tailored marketing strategy that puts them in front of potential clients who will not only value their services but also become raving fans.

The fundamental mistake new coaches often make is trying to be *everything to everyone*.

Your services will not resonate with everyone no matter whether you are targeting individuals or organisations. Defining your target audience is the most important step, as we have discussed in Chapter 1, and it is the starting point in any marketing plan.

Your target audience will also significantly influence your marketing channels, messaging and even service offerings.

Before diving into creating a marketing plan, it is important to understand the channels available to you. These could range from social media platforms, blogs and email newsletters to webinars, podcasts, traditional media, direct mail and networking events.

Understanding Marketing Channels

There are many different marketing channels, and some will work better than others for your business. Before you dismiss any of them, have an open mind.

Newspapers are still great for older audiences. TV can be done more creatively through product placement. Think outside the box. How could you team up with some other local businesses for National Small Business Day and split the cost?

SWAP, Marketing Without Money by Therese Tarlinton is a great book about partnerships and collaborations that might get you thinking about creative solutions.

Before you start seeing all the shiny objects and the glimmering stars, read this whole chapter. Here are some types of marketing channels that you can consider using.

Notice I said, "consider". Start with 1 or 2, then build on more later. Repurposing content is a great way to spread your message across multiple platforms without having to start from scratch.

Your Website

In today's digital world, having a solid online presence is essential. Your website serves as the home base for all your marketing activities. Think of your website as your digital headquarters, your office, the go-to place for your coaching services. Make sure it clearly communicates your value proposition, includes client testimonials and offers valuable content through blogs or videos. Allow your clients to schedule calls, buy your programs and contact you easily. All these elements work together to establish your expertise and trustworthiness.

Search Engine Optimisation (SEO) should be a priority, helping potential clients find you when they are searching for the solutions you offer. A well-optimised website will appear in relevant search results, increasing the likelihood that your ideal clients will find you rather than you having to seek them out.

Remember, along with looking good, your website should serve as an effective tool for converting curious visitors into committed clients. Don't just create a website to tick a box; make it a central part of your marketing strategy.

Testimonials from happy clients are your best marketing assets. Encourage satisfied customers to leave testimonials, which you can feature prominently on your website and social media. Word-of-mouth referrals can be incredibly impactful, so don't shy away from asking for them.

Don't be tempted to skip having a website in favour of building your business on a social media platform instead. Many businesses have lost all their customers overnight when their social media accounts have been shut down, often through no fault of their own. You would spend thousands of dollars renovating a home that you were only renting. Don't build your digital home on a platform that you don't own and have little control over and that can't be searched. Social media should be a valuable part of your marketing plan; however, it should not be your whole marketing plan.

Social Media

Social media platforms offer a fantastic way to reach a broad audience without breaking the bank. Social platforms like LinkedIn are for business professionals, Facebook has a broader audience and Instagram is more visual and has a younger demographic. Determine which platforms your ideal clients frequent and focus your efforts there. Use these platforms to showcase your expertise and connect with potential clients. These are only some of the platforms available.

When social platforms are used well, they enable you to showcase your brand and knowledge, share client testimonials, be a guest leveraging other people's audience and even give live coaching tips.

Social media can be a double-edged sword. For the most part, the platforms are free. However, they can be a huge time suck, full of exciting rabbit holes, and many have a big learning curve. Be mindful of where your target audience spends most of their time and focus your efforts there. Crafting a social media calendar can help you maintain consistency and measure the impact of your campaigns. More on content calendars in Chapter 7.

Don't be busy, for the sake of being busy, and call it marketing.

Blogs and Articles

Writing high-quality, valuable content positions you as an expert in your field, or on a chosen topic, and can attract more visitors to your website. Write blog posts that solve common problems your target audience faces, and make videos offering quick tips, which can then be transcribed and turned into an article. These articles can draw organic traffic to your website and can provide valuable content that you can repurpose and share across other channels. Content marketing is a long-term strategy but one that establishes trust and credibility like no other. Blog articles are searchable and a great thing to add to your regular marketing plan.

Webinars and Podcasts

Hosting or guesting on webinars and podcasts can help you reach a new and wider audience. These mediums allow you to explore subjects in a deeper, more meaningful way, offer more comprehensive advice and build trust by providing tangible value to listeners. Webinars and podcasts provide value in a format that is easy for listeners to consume.

Email Newsletters

Email remains one of the most effective marketing channels and is often underestimated. Email newsletters are a direct line to interested clients and offer you the space to send more in-depth information, updates and offers directly to their inbox. Collect email addresses through your website, offering a free eBook or a newsletter subscription as an incentive. You can use this list to nurture relationships, provide additional value and occasionally promote your services or special offers.

Traditional Media

Newspapers, radio and TV spots. Though often more expensive, these channels can still provide a wide reach and lend a level of credibility to your coaching service. Local newspapers and community radio often have loyal followings. If they match your ideal audience, that could be a cost-effective way to reach them.

Direct Mail

Sending tailored material through post might seem old-fashioned, but it is a personalised way to capture attention. A personalised direct mail piece can make your potential clients feel valued.

The days of blanket direct mail are gone for small businesses. However, there are many creative ways to get attention in an uncrowded mailbox. Think about what you normally get in the mail: mainly bills if you haven't changed them to email yet. Direct mail can be by post or courier.

Example

Jon Blake, who is a sales coach, has lots of different examples. Here are 2.

He had a local florist deliver a punnet of cherry tomatoes with his marketing material to a CEO, who loved tomatoes, to get attention. If you are a wellness coach looking to do corporate wellness workshops, what could you have delivered?

Another example was a sales coach having an empty golf bag delivered with the message "Work with me and I will get you so many sales that you will have more time to play golf."

Personalised direct mail is very powerful.

Networking Events

People like to do business with people. The power of a personal connection has never been more important. Whether it is through industry events, seminars or even social functions, face to face interactions offer valuable networking opportunities. Networking provides the chance to make lasting impressions and can often lead to valuable word-of-mouth referrals. Making meaningful relationships with other coaches can especially be a great source of referrals.

Example

A friend of mine is a leadership coach. A potential client approached her after a speaking gig. After a short discussion, she could clearly see that the client needed help with her marketing, not her leadership skills. My friend recommended me because I am a marketing coach.

Another friend who is a coach established a relationship with the leading executive coach in her area and now gets referrals from that coach's overflow clients.

Public Relations and Media Appearances

Depending on your niche and expertise, opportunities may exist for media appearances, interviews or contributions to articles. These can significantly boost your credibility and provide exposure to a much larger audience. Be proactive in seeking these opportunities, and make sure to prepare adequately when they do come up. Websites like SourceBottle.com or Haro.com are good places to start looking for PR opportunities.

Marketing Without an Online Presence

In today's digital landscape, having an online presence is like having a business card; it is essential.

Can you develop a coaching business without going online?

Yes, you can. Traditional methods of getting clients, like word-of-mouth referrals, networking events and partnerships, are very valuable. However, not utilising the power of the online world could mean missing out on a wealth of opportunities, making your marketing efforts so much harder. Your online channels can put you in front of hundreds, if not thousands, of your ideal customers with a few clicks of a button.

Your potential clients are already online, searching for solutions to their problems, the solutions that you can provide. If you are not visible, you can bet your competitors are, and then who will these potential clients find? A well-crafted online presence can help you reach a wider audience, educate and engage with them in a meaningful way, establish your brand and even set the stage for a global client base.

You can develop a coaching business without going online. However, you are making it harder for yourself and will need to find other ways to get in front of your target audience.

Example

I have a coaching client who has an extremely successful coaching practice with a very minimal social presence. She has a huge network and email list. Anytime she needs to increase her workload, all she has to do is reach out to her existing network and make an offer.

If you have a large email list or social network, you may be able to introduce your new coaching services to them. Please stay within the privacy laws of your country. If the database was collected from another business or purpose, you cannot use it to advertise your new services. If in doubt—don't.

By understanding these marketing channels, you will be better equipped to choose the ones that will most effectively reach your target audience and help you grow your coaching business.

> *"Focus on building the best possible business. If you are great, people will notice and opportunities will appear."*
> *Mark Cuban*

Activity, Should You Choose to Accept!

This chapter has filled your toolbox with new marketing ideas. STOP. Wait, this is not a shiny object festival. Start with 1 or 2 and don't spread yourself too thin.

What is the first tool you are keen to try out? The chapter is about taking concentrated action that works for your business not just following the crowd.

Completing these exercises will help you to decide.

1. **What Are the Ways You Would Like to Market Your Business?**
   Write down a list of all the different ways that you can market your business. Use the Ways to Market worksheet to help you.

2. **Choose Your Marketing Channel.**
   Choose 2 channels to focus on first.

   - What type of content do you need for these channels?
   - Write 5 FAQs that you can answer for your audience.

3. **Check Out Extra Resources:**
   For more detailed exercises and tools that can help you decide on which marketing channel to start with, head over to cathysmith.com.au/book-resources.

State of the Art Tools

Amidst the vast expanse of the North Atlantic Ocean, the formidable USS Endeavor cut through the waves like a knife through butter. As the most advanced naval ship in its fleet, it boasted state-of-the-art technology, and its crew held immense pride in their vessel.

One evening, under a starless sky, the mood on the ship was relaxed as it sailed through familiar waters. Lieutenant Dan, one of the ship's younger officers, was at the helm. As he scanned the horizon, a faint light, twinkling like a distant star, caught his attention. The light appeared to be on a collision course with the USS Endeavor.

Following protocol, Lieutenant Dan radioed the source of the light, requesting it to change its course, 20 degrees to starboard. The response came back, "No. You need to move 20 degrees to your starboard."

The response was as puzzling as it was firm.

Uncertain and flustered, Dan felt the weight of this responsibility and decided to wake Captain Roberts, a seasoned leader known for his unwavering resolve. Grumbling slightly about being roused, the captain assessed the situation. He decided to take charge, firmly believing his position and rank would resolve the issue.

The captain boomed down the radio to the other ship to move starboard, 20 degrees, at once.

The other ship refused and told the captain once again that he should move his ship starboard, 20 degrees, at once.

"I am a captain of the US Navy, and I am commanding you to comply with my request. What rank are you?"

"Able seaman, Sir. However, I strongly suggest that you do change your course 20 degrees to starboard, Sir," was the reply.

By now the captain was becoming furious. How dare an able seaman refuse to follow his instructions?

"Son, you understand that I am a captain of one of the largest warships in the US Navy, and I am commanding you to change your course."

"Yes, sir, I do understand.

I'm a lighthouse. Your call."

The room went silent. The enormity of the near blunder weighed heavy in the air. They had almost steered a billion-dollar naval ship into a catastrophe because of an assumption.

Just as in the tale of the USS Endeavor and the lighthouse, assumptions and miscommunications can lead us astray. In the coaching realm, assuming you know exactly what a client needs without truly understanding their journey is akin to the ship's captain not realising he was communicating with a lighthouse. It can lead to disastrous results.

For a coach, the tools and techniques in their arsenal are crucial. However, they are effective only when used with precision and understanding. A lighthouse won't change its position no matter how formidable the ship confronting it. Similarly, a coaching program can't be effective if it is not tailored to the unique needs, positions, and challenges of a specific client or client type.

Drawing from the story, just as the captain needed to adjust the ship's course after understanding the true nature of the "obstacle" ahead, a coach must also understand the client's obstacles and articulate how your coaching will help them. Some clients will not be a good fit, and referring them to another coach is the best course of action for you both.

Remember, it is not about having the most tools or the grandest ship; it is about knowing when, where, and how to use them effectively.

Now that you have the who and where, keep going to Chapter 7 to work on the how: creating a marketing strategy. Having a marketing strategy makes your marketing so much easier because you have a map to follow, and all your decisions will be governed by that map.

Chapter 7

Marketing Magic to Find Clients Who Love You

You have got the skills, the brand and the passion to make a difference in people's lives. The question now is how do you get those people through your virtual (or physical) door? Marketing, when done well, is not about convincing people to buy something they don't need; it is about connecting the right individuals with the solutions you offer.

Every coach possesses a unique skill set, methodology and specialisation. Some may focus on life transitions or on executive leadership, while others specialise in relationships or personal growth, and these are still all broad areas. Recognising your niche and tailoring your messaging accordingly is vital. Your niche will attract your ideal potential clients. As discussed in Chapters 2 and 3, it will help you to establish your clear brand identity and the future of your coaching business.

Now, you need to go out and find clients who will love you. When you have done your marketing well, your clients will find you. To begin, start by creating a marketing plan that you can follow so that you don't stray from your objective.

Planning Your Marketing Strategy

A comprehensive marketing plan serves as your roadmap to reach your target audience effectively.

1. **Identify Your Target Audience:** Knowing who you are marketing to will shape your messaging and the channels you will use. Go back to Chapter 2 to craft your identity and 6 to lay the groundwork of where to find your ideal audience if you haven't completed these exercises yet.

2. **Set Objectives:** Whether it is gaining 10 new clients in the next quarter or getting your first client. Setting measurable goals is essential.

3. **Choose Marketing Channels:** Select the channels that will most effectively reach your target audience.

4. **Budget and Resources:** Allocate your budget and resources based on the channels you have chosen. Remember, this can be money and/or time. You will need to allocate time to be able to create marketing that will work for you.

5. **Implementation:** Execute your marketing strategies consistently. Consistency is the key to all good marketing because your potential clients may need many touchpoints before making the decision to work with you.

6. **Review:** Testing and measuring are essential. Regularly revisit your plan to adjust as needed. You don't want to continue a paid marketing campaign that is not producing results. However, if you continue to chop and change your marketing, you will end up frustrated and have little to show for your efforts. Data and strategy are key to successful marketing.

Creating a Marketing Plan

Navigating the complexities of building a thriving coaching business can be daunting, especially when it comes to marketing. But don't worry! A well-planned marketing strategy can serve as your roadmap, leading you straight to your ideal clients.

This roadmap consists of four pivotal steps:

- Research
- Ideas
- Planning
- Action

Each step is designed to take you closer to a marketing strategy that will capture the attention of and create genuine connections with people who need your coaching expertise. By following this roadmap, you will have what you need to create a rewarding and prosperous coaching journey.

Here is how you can approach each of these critical steps on your marketing roadmap:

Step 1 – Research

Before any marketing campaign, it is vital to understand your audience, your competition and the market landscape.

- Listen to what your potential clients are saying.
- Who have you already worked with? What was their feedback?
- What gap in the market can you see?

This step will help you tailor your marketing strategy to the exact needs and pain points of your target audience. Don't get stuck in analysis paralysis. You can refine it as you go along. Done is better than perfect. Just start.

Side note: don't commit to a shiny object marketing package if you haven't got your ideal customer and avatar nailed down first.

Step 2 – Ideas

Once you have ample research, it is time to brainstorm some innovative marketing ideas that align with your brand and objectives. This could involve creative advertising concepts, compelling content themes or out-of-the-box partnership opportunities. The goal is to think of fresh ways to engage your target audience while showcasing your unique value as a coach.

Step 3 – Planning

After brainstorming comes the structuring of your ideas into a coherent marketing plan. Outline your goals, the channels you will use and the resources you will need. Break down your ideas into actionable tasks and set realistic timelines for each. A well-organised plan will serve as the roadmap for your marketing success.

Step 4 – Action

Finally, it is time to execute your carefully crafted marketing plan. Consistency is key here. Whether it is posting regularly on social media or sending out monthly newsletters, ensure that you are continually putting your plan into practice. Monitor the results closely, adjusting your actions based on the feedback and data you collect.

By following this roadmap—Research, Ideas, Planning, and Action—you will be well on your way to creating a marketing strategy that positions you perfectly in front of your ideal clients.

Measuring ROI

The success of your marketing plan hinges on the Return on Investment (ROI) it delivers.

While ROI is commonly associated with financial gains, it is equally important to measure the return on your time. Paid marketing campaigns require not only a financial investment but also a commitment of time and effort to set up, monitor and tweak.

On the other side, organic methods like social media engagement or content creation may not cost much financially, but they can be time consuming. Understanding the ROI for both paid marketing and your time can provide invaluable insights. It helps you identify which strategies are most effective, allowing you to allocate your resources of both money and time more efficiently.

- **Track Metrics:** Use analytics tools to track metrics related to your goals, such as engagement rates, conversion rates, and overall reach. Be strategic and don't just boost a post because Facebook says so.

- **Cost Analysis:** Evaluate the cost involved in each marketing channel against the results it produces to assess its effectiveness.

- **Adjust and Iterate:** Based on your ROI, fine-tune your approach. Discontinue strategies that are not getting results and double down on those that are.

By understanding marketing channels, creating a robust marketing plan and consistently measuring ROI, you will be well-equipped to attract clients who need your services and are a joy to work with.

*"Good marketing allows your potential
customers to see what you are selling.
Great marketing makes them want to buy.
Exceptional marketing makes YOU the only option."
Cathy Smith*

Activity, Should You Choose to Accept!

There was a lot to think about in this chapter.

Where are you going to start? What is the first marketing channel that you are going to use?

Taking action is a must so that you will continue to move forward to create the business of your dreams.

1. **Take Your 2 Chosen Marketing Channels from Chapter 6.**
   Now it is time to plan out how you will use these marketing channels.
   Your content needs to be client focused and engaging.

   Write or record the text or script for 2 pieces of content.

2. **Create a 30 Day Marketing Plan.**
   Break it down week by week and include different marketing channels such as social media, email and offline events. Set specific, measurable goals for each.

3. **Check Out Extra Resources:**
   For more detailed exercises and tools that can help you decide which marketing channel to start with, head over to cathysmith.com.au/book-resources.

Fishing and Marketing

My husband is a keen fisherman. His love of fishing started very early as he spent time with his grandfather at the river and the beach learning all about how the fish behave and how they like to live. Granddad Pop was a product of the Great Depression, so although he didn't believe in catch and release, he was a great advocate for only taking what you need.

His lessons included the correct bait to use, going at the optimum time, making sure you have the right tackle for the species of fish you were going to target and knowing what type of fish were in your local area and their habits. He spent many hours showing my husband the ropes and skilling him in all things fishing. These skills have served my husband well, and he is often able to catch fish when many others do not.

We were walking on the beach one day and saw some people fishing off the sand a little way ahead. "They won't be catching any fish," my husband said.

He struck up a conversation with them. "How is the fishing going?"

"We were doing alright when we first got here but not so good now," they said.

They chatted about the bait and conditions for a bit, and then we continued on our walk.

"How did you know they weren't catching anything?" I asked.

"They are casting too far out. They are completely missing where the fish are!"

When we came back from our walk the fishermen were still there. As we approached my husband spotted a "bait ball", a spot where the baitfish are being herded into a circle by bigger fish.

"See the bait ball? Cast closer to the shore, in that gutter," he said, pointing, as we walked past.

The fisherman cast his line right into the middle of the baitfish and within seconds he had caught a fish. Quickly he re-baited and cast again, once again he quickly caught another fish.

Marketing Is a Lot Like Fishing

You need to know where your audience is, who your ideal people are and what type of "bait" serves them best.

Unfortunately, most business owners and coaches market like our fishing friends, all over the place and often overshooting where their market is.

When you use the wrong bait and fish in the wrong areas, you waste your time and money. Marketing is just the same; you often spend too much money in all the wrong areas, which is why most people think marketing is too hard and too expensive. Attracting your ideal audience requires intention and precision, just like a seasoned fisherman who studies the water and understands the habits of the fish. You need to delve deep into understanding your audience's preferences, behaviours and needs. Craft your message specifically for them, ensuring it resonates and offers genuine solutions to their challenges. By being strategic, focusing on your target, and using the right tools, you will not only save on resources but also reel in the audience that truly values what you offer. Remember, it is not about casting the widest net but about ensuring every catch aligns with your vision and purpose.

Congratulations on successfully navigating Chapter 7, where you have laid the foundation of your marketing strategy. This is a significant step towards turning your coaching passion into a thriving business. As you transition into Chapter 8, "Magnetising Your Ideal Client," you are ready to delve deeper into attracting the clients who will most benefit from your unique coaching style.

Chapter 8

Magnetising Your Ideal Client

The lifeblood of any coaching practice is the clients who bring their challenges, hopes and aspirations through your door, whether virtually or literally. Your ability to magnetise your ideal client will fuel your business and ensure a rewarding and impactful coaching journey for both you and the client.

Where to Find Clients

Clients are everywhere.

Yet finding the right ones, those perfect matches for your coaching services, requires a strategic approach. As discussed, many times throughout this book, everyone is not your client.

In Chapter 6, "Laying the Groundwork to Attract Your Ideal Audience," we looked at your marketing channels and many places to find your ideal clients and how to reach them.

The Marketing Funnel for Coaches

The marketing funnel is not just a buzzword. It is a framework that helps you understand your customer's journey from being a complete stranger to becoming a loyal client. For coaches, the funnel typically starts with awareness. This could be a social media post, a blog or word of mouth. The next stage involves engaging your audience through targeted content, webinars or free sessions.

Your funnel narrows as you move towards conversion or purchase, the crucial point where a potential client decides to take the plunge and engage your services. Don't overlook the post-conversion stage. A satisfied client can become your biggest advocate, propelling your funnel by generating referrals and positive reviews.

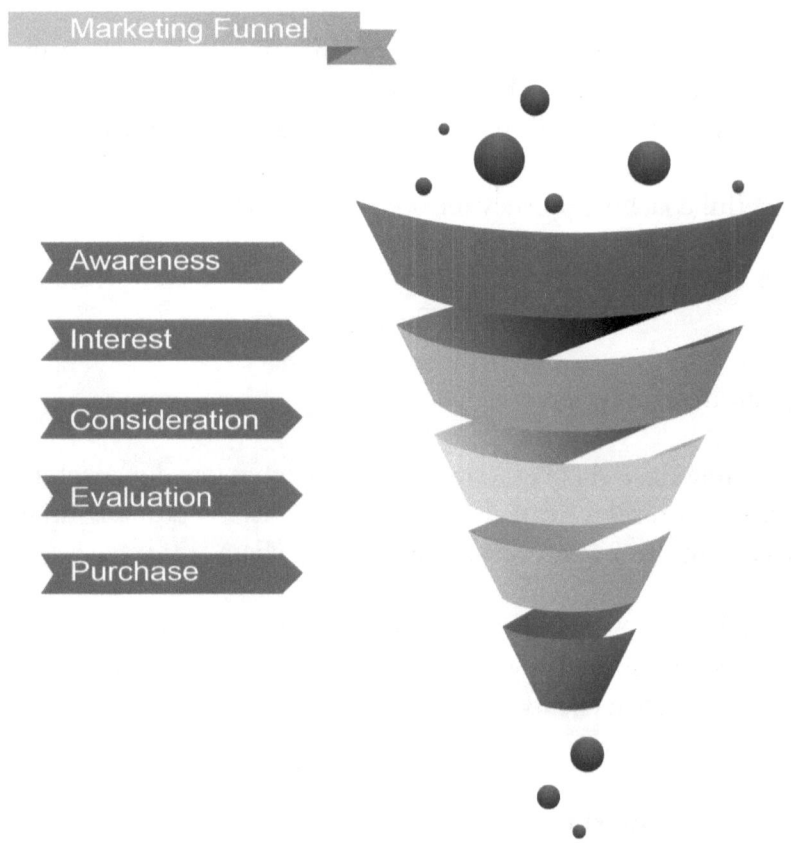

The Initial Contact

The initial contact with a potential client is critical as it sets the tone for the entire coaching relationship. The first contact will often happen without you being present. A well-crafted email or direct message can capture their attention right from the start. When doing direct messages, make sure to personalise the message and state clearly why you are reaching out to them.

We have all had the experience of accepting a LinkedIn connection and then having our inbox filled with a novel's worth of "buy my stuff". Not a nice experience and a total waste of time for everyone.

If you would not do it in person, then don't do it on socials either. No one asks for a kiss the minute you meet someone, so don't push your coaching on anyone without even having a conversation.

First impressions are lasting impressions, and you want to kick off the relationship on a high note. You are a coach. You are here to help people and make a difference, and your marketing should reflect that too, no matter how much you need a new client.

Scarcity and lack are not good emotions to start a new coaching relationship with. Starting a new coaching relationship with feelings of scarcity or lack can set a negative tone that is hard to shake off. When you approach potential clients from this mindset, there is a risk of seeming desperate or pushy, which can erode trust before you have even begun working together. Clients are more likely to invest in you when they sense that you are motivated by a genuine desire to help them achieve their goals, rather than an urgent need to make a sale and get paid.

If you are operating from a mindset of scarcity, you will be more inclined to compromise on the quality of your services or take on clients who are not an ideal fit for you. It is crucial to build your coaching practice on a foundation of abundance, confidence, and a genuine commitment to making a positive impact.

Know, Like and Trust

We like to do business with people we know, like and trust. That is why word of mouth referrals are so valuable, as the trust is implied by the person referring you.

Add Value First

An effective approach is to offer something of value upfront, such as a free eBook, webinar or sample coaching session (that is different from the consult, see Chapter 9). This provides a low-barrier entry point to your services, allowing the potential client to experience your expertise without any risk.

To create a successful client interaction, start by offering them something of value that addresses a specific need or problem they have. This initial gesture can provide immediate relief and establish your credibility. Once you have captured their interest, collect their email address to continue the conversation and provide even more tailored solutions.

Don't underestimate the power of social engagement. Commenting on relevant posts, sharing your own perspectives, adding value and introducing yourself in community threads can make your presence known and build initial rapport. Your intention should always be to give without expectation and add value.

1. Give them something of value.
2. Collect email address.
3. Solve their problem.
4. Give them a way to buy from you.

This can be summarised as Opt-in, Value, Offer.

Your ultimate goal should be to solve their problem in a way that proves the value of your services. By doing so, you pave the way for the client to purchase from you. Essentially, the process involves a seamless transition from opt-in to providing value and, finally, to making an offer they cannot refuse.

Giving Away too Much for Free

When you first start out, doing some free sample coaching sessions can be a good strategy to get some practice with real clients and start to establish relationships. Free sessions can also be offered in exchange for a testimonial. However, you are running a business, and giving away all your services for free will not create the success and income that you need for a thriving business.

Often, a better strategy is to start with a low price point and increase it every time you have booked 2 or 4 clients at that rate. Go back to Chapter 5, "Setting Your Price for Success", if you have not read it yet or need a refresher.

The Art of Client Retention

Client attraction is just the first step. To build a sustainable coaching practice, you also need to be able to enable your prospects to become clients and then retain them. Having a steady flow of new and repeat clients means you are creating a thriving coaching practice.

Often, coaches spend a lot of time and effort reaching out to new people. However, the gold is in doing a fabulous job, helping your clients have transformations and then helping them with the next step in the journey.

> *"New level, new devil."*
> *Denise Duffield-Thomas*

You may be able to offer a new or more advanced service as your client achieves their first transformation.

Customisation is key to an unforgettable client experience. From remembering significant milestones in your client's life to tailoring coaching materials to suit individual learning styles, personal touches make your service stand out.

Value = Price. The more value you can offer, the bigger the transformation, the higher the price and the more good you can do in the world.

Not All Clients Are Ready to Buy

At any one time, only 2–5% of potential clients are ready to buy your services.

That is 95% of your potential audience who are not ready yet, and some will never be ready.

60–80% of all sales require more than 4 touchpoints or ways to follow up. A client who is in the thinking stage may need up to 20 touchpoints before they have evaluated all options and are ready to buy. These touchpoints can be over many months or in a matter of minutes.

Think about the way you buy when you are looking for a new product or service.

Example

If your fridge breaks down and you need a new one, the sales cycle is compressed to who has one in stock and when it can be delivered the quickest. I bought a black fridge because it was the only one of the type that I wanted that was in stock and available to be delivered that day. I was leaving on holiday the following day and couldn't leave the house sitters without a fridge.

If you are looking to replace an existing fridge because you are moving into a new home in a few months that has a cream kitchen instead of a white one, then your sales cycle can be much longer. You will have time to research, price check and wait for delivery.

Coaching services can be the same. It depends on the urgency of the problem and whether the client has been researching before they came across you.

Nurturing new prospects and existing clients is very important for your business to thrive. Having a value-add email sequence or newsletter to go out to your database can provide great touchpoints.

Clear Communication Is Key

Tailor your communications and proposals to address the specific needs and goals of clients is important, especially if you are offering 1 on 1 coaching. Always be clear about what your coaching program includes, your policies, pricing, cancellations and any other terms and conditions. Transparency fosters trust and reduces the risk of any misunderstandings later.

The Importance of Relationship Building in The Sales Cycle

Building a strong relationship starts the moment a potential client encounters your brand. Whether it is through a referral, an online article or a social media post, this initial contact sets the stage for trust. Relationship building doesn't stop once the client signs on. It continues to evolve, providing a strong foundation for long-term loyalty and advocacy. Past clients who have had the transformation you offer are often your best referrals.

Building relationships is at the heart of coaching. Regular check-ins, active listening and showing that you genuinely care can go a long way.

As you don't know where your prospects are in their buying cycle or customer journey, nurturing them is a great way to make sure no one gets left behind at your first pit stop. Nurturing your clients and prospects serves as the extra layer of attention that distinguishes you from the competition. Continual engagement through educational content, special offers and the occasional update of product offerings shows that you care. Being invested in their progress and looking after your audience is an easy way to set yourself apart from your competitors.

This feedback loop creates a win-win scenario. Your audience of clients and prospects feel heard and valued, and you gain insights that help you refine your coaching services. This way, you will maintain strong relationships and foster a community of advocates who are likely to refer your services to others.

The Art of Client Retention

Great client experiences are created with your whole package. From your booking system to your session environment, every touchpoint contributes to the client experience. Make it as seamless, supportive and value laden as you possibly can.

One of the first tangible interactions a client will have with you is booking a session. Make this process as smooth and hassle-free as possible. Whether it is an online system or a phone in booking, aim for efficiency. Send calendar reminders or confirmation messages to reassure clients that their time is reserved and valued. In our busy lives reminders are appreciated and will reduce the no-show rate.

Handling Objections

Even in the most promising coaching relationships, objections and hurdles can arise. Whether it is doubt about the process or concern about the price, your ability to address these objections with grace and clarity is crucial.

This is a normal part of the process. You have not done anything wrong, and it doesn't make you a bad coach. Concentrate on the things that you are doing well and amplify them.

Sometimes objections are based on misunderstandings or a need for clarification. Ask questions of your client to get to the root of the issue. See Chapter 11, "Turning 'No' Into 'Yes' for Client Success," for more suggestions on how to handle objections and to minimise them.

If you have done something wrong, communication is the key. Then dust yourself off and move on to helping someone else.

Magnetising Your Ideal Client for a Thriving Coaching Business

The end goal is to attract clients, retain some of them and build a thriving coaching practice that changes lives, including your own. Keep these principles in mind as you navigate the journey of client attraction and retention.

By focusing on these aspects of client experience, you are not just selling a service; you are providing an experience that can turn one-time clients into loyal advocates for your coaching business.

An excellent client experience is a blend of professional knowledge, emotional intelligence and operational efficiency, all aimed at exceeding client expectations and setting you apart in a crowded marketplace.

> *"Don't be intimidated by what you don't know.*
> *That can be your greatest strength and ensure that you do things differently from everyone else."*
> *Sara Blakely*

Activity, Should You Choose to Accept!

As you can see, each chapter is building on the one before. Are you also building on your business? Have you got your systems organised?

1. **Sort Out Your Systems.**
   A basic thing you will need is a booking system with payment. What are you using for your calendar and payments?

   Your task for this chapter is to find a system that suits you. There are many free or cheap options; make sure that they can grow with you as you don't want to have to do it all again when your business takes off. Don't overextend yourself either. Get what you need now with some room for growth.

The Supercar Strategy: A Lesson in Timing and Adaptability for Client Attraction

In July, Australian Supercar Racing arrived in Perth. As you have probably worked out by now, I love cars, driving and car racing. Supercars, resembling road production cars, tear around a bitumen track at speeds up to 220km/h. Wanneroo, Perth's purpose-built track, spanning 2.7km with 7 turns, offers few passing opportunities, making the races very strategic. Supercars is an exciting form of motorsport with all the glitz and glamour.

Races typically cover 32 laps, with average lap times of just over a minute, dropping below in sprints. The strategy intensifies with mandatory pit stops for tyre changes. These stops, lasting 3-8 seconds, are crucial for maintaining top speeds, as the cars use slick tyres for maximum performance.

The final race is always thrilling, with championship points at stake. Team strategies, tyre changes and passing manoeuvres. In one race, while one team pitted early to gain track advantage, the other delayed their stop. This tactic seemed risky until an accident led to a safety car deployment, equalising the field.

Once racing resumed, the team with fresher tyres outpaced their rivals, clinching victory. This race was not only about speed but also about strategic timing and adaptability. These same qualities are essential in attracting and retaining coaching clients.

In coaching, like in racing, strategy is key. Coaches must decide when to introduce new offerings to engage potential clients. This approach is like changing tyres in racing for better performance. Market shifts, resembling the safety car in racing, provide opportunities to reassess and adapt strategies.

Client relationships, much like a race, are built over time, requiring multiple touchpoints for conversion. A successful coaching business, therefore, mirrors a well-planned racing strategy, requiring foresight and an understanding of the market. These parallels highlight the importance of strategic planning in both racing and coaching.

What Next?

You have reached out and have a few potential clients. Now it is time to get them on a call and offer your services. In Chapter 9, we will talk about the consult and how to have those sales conversations without feeling icky.

Chapter 9

Mastering the Art of Client Conversion

For many coaches, the idea of having to "sell" feels icky and intimidating. You may have an incredible coaching service to offer, but if you can't sell it, you will struggle to make your business viable.

No sales = no business = expensive hobby.

The bottom line is if you cannot or will not sell your services, then there is no possible way to make your business thrive. STOP reading this book right now as you are wasting your time, and go and find a paid job.

Embracing this shift in perspective and realising that sales are essential to be profitable is a pivotal moment that will transform your coaching practice from a hobby into a thriving business. Viewing sales as meaningful conversations opens the door to more authentic and productive interactions with potential clients. You can now approach these sales conversations not just as an obligation but as a core aspect of your daily operations, helping you to assist your clients and create the business of your dreams.

Sales Conversations

Try thinking of selling as a conversation. You are having a chat to see how you can help the potential client then offering ways that you can help and allowing them to buy these services, which will solve their problem. If you have the cure to their problem, isn't it your duty to offer it to them and allow the client to buy it or not?

Sales conversations should be part of every coach's day-to-day life.

You are not just "selling" your service; you are offering a transformation, a new beginning. Approach sales talks as if they are coaching sessions:

- Be curious.
- Ask questions.
- Above all, listen.

Understand your client's pain points and articulate clearly how your coaching can offer a solution.

Remember, your role in a sales conversation is 2-fold:

1. To provide clarity. Often the client will need help to articulate the problem.
2. To guide a decision.

Whether the client says "yes" or "no" is irrelevant at this stage, as you are only helping them with those 2 things, clarity and decision-making.

Although you should treat this conversation with a coaching mindset, do not fall into the trap of thinking it is a coaching session. You are not here to fix their problem, only to help the client realise what the problem is and that you have the solution. If you do fix their problem, they are likely to do 1 of 2 things:

1. Think you are amazing then leave and never come back.
2. Continue to ask you to fix other problems for free.

Coaching is not about high-pressure tactics, sales scripts or coercing people into services they don't want. That is not why we became coaches.

If you align your service to your client's needs, the sale will naturally follow as a mere formality at the end of the conversation. Remember, if they don't inquire about the next steps, you will need to add it to the conversation and ask.

I have really enjoyed our conversation today, and the next step to create this transformation for you is _____. How does that sound?

Successfully moving prospective clients into loyal customers is not just about making a sale; it is about integrating the client seamlessly into your coaching practice and beginning a transformational journey for both of you.

Navigating the Sales Process

Let's shift gears and look at the bigger picture: the whole sales process.

You see, selling isn't an isolated event but a natural progression of conversations that should be in your everyday toolkit as a coach.

The sales process is more than just a transaction. It is a series of well-planned interactions that guide the client from awareness to decision. It is about understanding your client's needs and presenting your services as the ideal solution. By mastering this process, you are stepping through a series of talks designed to help your prospective clients make a choice that serves them best.

The steps, when you break them down, are not so different from a coaching session:

1. **Initial Interaction**: This is your meet and greet. Whether it is a call, an email or a chance meeting at a conference, it is a casual chat to see if there is a fit. Your only task here is to gauge interest and secure a time for a deeper dive, a consult.

2. **The Consult**: This is the heart-to-heart. You get to really listen, ask specific questions and understand their aspirations and challenges. Be that guide who helps them articulate what the problem really is.

3. **Offering Solutions**: Based on the heart-to-heart, you have a tailored solution to share. Now, you are not just suggesting a coaching package; you are offering a pathway to transformation. Lay it out for them, step by step. Revisit Chapter 4 if you have not worked out your starter package yet.

4. **Addressing the "But What Ifs"**: Ah, objections. These are not roadblocks but signposts that you are getting to the real issues. Treat them as questions begging for answers. They want to say yes; they just need a bit more clarity to get there.

5. **The Decision Moment**: At this point, it is about making a choice. Remember your role is only 2 fold? Offer clarity and guide the decision. It is not about pushing but facilitating a decision that serves them.

6. **The After Chat**: Even when the formal conversations or coaching sessions end, keep the communication lines open. A happy client is a repeat client and a walking, talking billboard for your services.

The Consult

Let's talk more about running a successful consult, a critical step that often serves as the cornerstone of your coaching relationship. At this stage, you get the chance to explore the heart of your prospective client's challenges, aspirations and goals. This consult is a 2-way street where you are not only assessing their needs but also demonstrating your value as a coach.

Listening Actively: As a coach, you already know that the first rule of any successful consult is to listen more than you talk. Active listening will allow you to pick up on subtle cues, whether verbal or nonverbal, that may reveal much about your prospective client's needs. This is both about hearing what is said and understanding what is left unsaid.

Asking the Right Questions: Good coaching starts with good questions. The questions you ask should be open-ended, encouraging your prospective client to share freely.

Ask a starter question. Remember not to stack questions; ask 1 question at a time and listen. Really listen. Don't just wait to ask your next question.

Example

- *Tell me a little bit about yourself.*
- *What would you like to chat about today?*
- *Can you tell me more about your current challenges?*
- *What made you reach out to me today?*

These questions open up a dialogue where you can identify both surface-level and deeper issues.

Understanding Aspirations: While it is important to understand the client's challenges, it is equally vital to grasp their aspirations. This not only provides a balanced view but also offers a direction for your coaching strategy. Knowing their goals can help you tailor your programs or solutions in a way that directly speaks to what they aim to achieve.

Defining the Problem: Many people struggle with a vague sense of dissatisfaction without being able to pinpoint the actual issue. As a coach, your role is crucial in helping them articulate this problem. Once you have clearly defined the problem, it becomes something you can work together to solve.

Being the Guide: Your role during the consult is like that of a guide. You are helping the prospective client navigate through a fog of thoughts, feelings and aspirations to arrive at a clearer understanding of what they truly need. By helping them articulate their problem clearly, you are already offering immense value.

Present Reality to Future Aspirations

As their guide, you need to show them the journey that you will take them on, turning their present reality into their future aspirations. You need to be able to identify the answers to these questions:

What is their problem?
What have they already tried that has not worked?
What is the real problem?
What is the real solution?
Why is change important to them?

The Wheel of Life is a great exercise to walk your clients through to enable them to answer these questions.

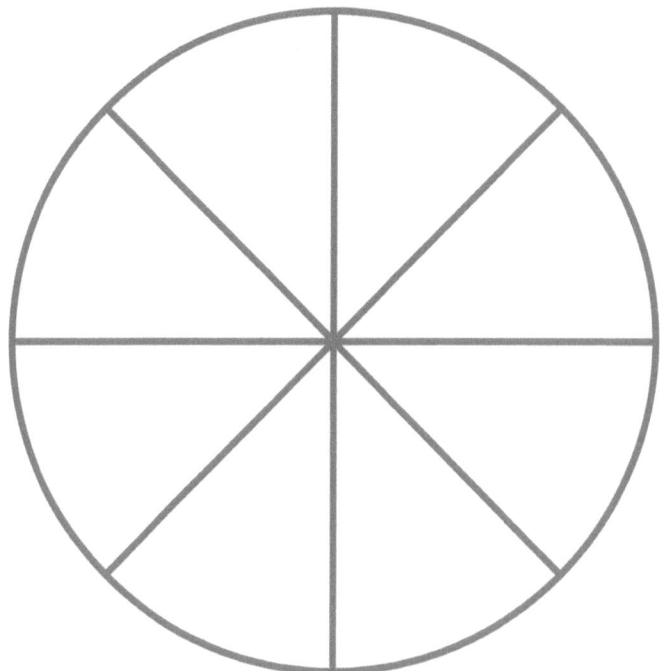

How to Use the Wheel:

Pick 6 to 8 areas of (your niche). Label them for your client. Then ask, "On a scale of 1-10, how would you rate your satisfaction in each area (e.g. life, career, business, future)?"

Why did you choose that score?
What past events made you choose that score?

What would need to change for it to be a 10?
What can you do in the future that is a different action to create a 10, as your score?

For full instructions on the wheel of life, see The Consult Worksheet in the resources at cathysmith.com.au/book-resources.

Laying the Groundwork for What Comes Next

The consult is not just a stand-alone event. Don't be tempted to coach and solve the problem that your client identified during the consult. The consult is an introduction to your coaching program, not your actual coaching.

It is your chance to outline how you work and what they can expect in terms of sessions, follow-ups and additional resources. If they are ready to take the next step, your consult should naturally guide them in that direction.

The consult is an opportunity to set the stage for a meaningful coaching relationship. By the end of it, both you and the client should have a clearer idea of how you can bring value to them through your coaching program, whether that be 1 on 1 coaching, a group program or other coaching options you offer.

The Sales Chat

Sales is only about having interactions. Every interaction holds its unique place and purpose, just like in coaching. And remember, you are not convincing; you are just having a conversation.

If the client sees the value in what you offer, the "yes" becomes a formality. Be clear about the next steps. If they don't ask, take the initiative, and bring how to work with you into the conversation. You are the guide, the expert, and often clients will wait for you to lead.

Example

"I've really enjoyed exploring possibilities with you today. As discussed, getting your marketing strategy planned out and implemented will really drive your coaching business forward. To get started on this transformational journey, the next step is to start on the 3 month 1 to 1 coaching plan that consists of 9 sessions. How does that sound to you?"

If they say "No", explore the objections. See Chapter 10, "Turning 'No' Into 'Yes' for Client Success" for tips for exploring the objections.

If "No" is definitely no, see Chapter 9, "Magnetising Your Ideal Client." No can quite often be not yet, and the client needs more touchpoints before deciding. Can you suggest a low-cost or free offering?

Thanks for your time today. You might like to check out my book, Coaches Marketing Roadmap, *or listen to my podcast,* Small Business Talk for Coaches, *which has lots of free marketing advice.*

Not everyone, no matter how perfect they seem, will be your client. Some clients need more touchpoints before they commit. For others, the consult is just a learning experience for you. Ask yourself what you can do differently next time. Don't beat yourself up or come from a place of scarcity that will not be helpful to anyone.

The Art of Overcoming Objections

Many potential clients will have hesitations or objections, whether they voice them or not. Your task is to understand these concerns and address them confidently and clearly. The best way to handle objections is through your marketing so that they have been answered before your person even gets on the call with you.

By answering objections, you will alleviate doubt and facilitate the client's own journey towards saying "yes" to the transformation you offer.

Let's be honest, rejection is often an inevitable part of sales. Not everyone you speak to is your ideal client, and you should not coach everyone. Sometimes you are not the right fit for this person's needs. The key is not to see rejection or a "No" as failure but as feedback. If a potential client decides not to proceed, it is an opportunity for you to learn and refine your approach.

Some common hurdles in sales conversations might include:

- Pricing.
- Commitment or time.
- Scepticism about the effectiveness of coaching.

Be prepared to explore their objections in more detail. Testimonials can help too. Have a backup plan, like a "starter package" that requires less commitment. See Chapter 10 for more tips on overcoming objections.

Mastering the Art of Client Conversion, the Sales Conversation

By mastering these techniques, you are learning how to align your coaching services more closely with the needs and desires of your future clients. Remember, the goal is client transformation, and the sale is simply the first step in that exciting journey.

As you continue your career in coaching, let this chapter serve as your guide in mastering the art of client conversion. Each section provides you with actionable steps that align closely with both the business and empathetic sides of your coaching practice.

> *"And if the end result is that someone, somewhere winds up believing they can do something out of the ordinary, well, then you have really made it."*
> *Angela Ahrendts*

Activity, Should You Choose to Accept!

Selling is not "icky". It is the first step to creating your client transformation and the beginning of an exciting journey. So, let's get started. Complete these exercises and then go for it. Go out, meet people and book a consult or 2.

1. **Complete The Consult Worksheet.**

   This worksheet gives you more information and suggestions on ways to run your consults.

   Answer the following questions:

   1. What do they think their problem is?
   2. What do they think the solution is?
   3. Where are they? Where do they want to be?
   4. What is missing?
   5. Actual problem / actual solution?
   6. How can you help?

2. **Try a Role-Playing Activity.**

   You might like to record a mock sales conversation with a friend playing a potential client. Listen to the recording and identify areas where you handled objections well and areas where you can improve.

How to Catch a Potential Customer's Eye

King Akbar lived a very boring life filled with the same court business day in and day out.

During the summer he thought of a way to make his life more interesting—he would ask his court a question every week and they would have to answer it. The winner would get a prize.

The first questions were simple. "What was my mother's name?" "What is my favourite meal?" And then King Akbar asked a question that no one in the court could answer.

While they deliberated, a man named Birbal walked in and asked what the matter was.

King Akbar asked him, "How many crows are there in the city?"

Birbal immediately smiled. He announced the answer right away: "There are twenty-one thousand, five hundred and twenty-three crows in the city."

"How do you know, Birbal?" the King asked.

Birbal replied, "You think I am wrong? Ask your men to count the number of crows. If there are more, then the relatives of the crows must be visiting them from nearby cities. If there are fewer, then the crows from our city must be visiting their relatives who live outside the city."

Pleased with such an interesting answer, Akbar presented Birbal with a ruby and pearl chain.

You are probably wondering, what does Birbal's clever answer have to do with sales conversion for coaches?

When you are in a consult or sales conversation, you don't always need to have a textbook answer ready. Use your listening skills and think on your feet. Offer a solution that resonates with your potential client. Just like Birbal, you can turn a challenging situation into an opportunity to shine. Next time you find yourself stuck in a tough sales conversation, think about what the client is really asking for and how you can be the solution to their problem. Be resourceful, be creative and show your potential clients that you have got the unique solutions they have been searching for. It will make all the difference. Sometimes the perfect solution is not to work together, and that is ok too. Refer them on and create a win for everyone.

Objections are a normal part of the sales process. Think of objections not as roadblocks but as signposts guiding you to the real issues.

Let's dive into Chapter 10, "Turning 'No' Into 'Yes' for Client Success." Once you have mastered that, you will be well on your way to having a thriving business.

Chapter 10

Turning "No" Into "Yes" for Client Success

Despite your best efforts, objections will arise. These could range from the price to the duration of the coaching program. What is important is not the objection itself, but how you handle it. Use this as an opportunity to listen, provide clarity and address their concerns. By doing so, you are aiming to both overcome a hurdle and also deepen your understanding of your client's needs.

The goal is to be curious and serve, never to try and make someone do something they don't want to.

Understanding the Nature of Objections

Ah, the "but what ifs", the objections. These are not roadblocks but signposts that you are getting to the real issues. Treat them as questions begging for answers. They want to say yes; they just need a bit more clarity to get there.

We often say "no" if we are scared or don't understand the process.

Active Listening and Empathy

Before trying to navigate the objection and go straight into a solution, it is vital to genuinely listen to the client's objection. Display empathy and make sure you fully comprehend the issue before attempting to counter it. Embrace the discomfort that objections bring; it is a sign that you are stepping into new territory. Sometimes, merely feeling heard can shift the client's perspective, making them more open to considering your services.

Instead of rushing your client towards a resolution, give them the space to fully express their concerns. Be present, actively listen and explore their objections with genuine curiosity.

Asking for permission to delve deeper into the issue not only shows respect but also opens the door for a more meaningful discussion. Once you have that permission, gently dig a little further to help them gain awareness of the underlying issues or fears that might be influencing their objections.

"Is the price your only concern, or are there other aspects you would like to discuss?"

This opens up a conversation, allowing you to address each point comprehensively.

Empower your clients by giving them the space to make a considered decision, rather than reacting impulsively. You can turn objections into opportunities for deeper understanding, stronger relationships and more informed choices.

Often objections are just asking for clarity. Explain it more. Show them the process.

If we COULD find a way to work together…would you want to?

No

If they say "No", then it is not an objection you can help with. Time to wish them well and end the call.

You could ask "Why"; feedback can be good.

Yes

Is it okay if I ask you a couple more questions?

If I could wave a magic wand and you did have (the money, time, permission), so all obstacles were gone, what would you decide and why?

Dealing with Client Objections

Being aware of potential common objections allows you to be prepared and helps you navigate concerns in a positive way and clear the path for a rewarding coaching experience.

Common objections often revolve around 5 main areas.

- **Price**: "Coaching is too expensive."
- **Permission**: "I need to talk to my spouse, business partner, etc."
- **Time**: "I don't have the time for coaching sessions."
- **Value**: "What will I gain from coaching?"
- **Commitment**: "I'm not sure if I can commit to a coaching program."

Strategies to Overcome Objections

Once you have identified these common objections, you can develop strategies to address them effectively. This proactive approach will build your confidence and empower you to guide prospective clients from scepticism to trust, setting the stage for a transformative coaching journey.

- **For Cost**: Offer flexible payment plans or emphasise the long term value and ROI (Return on Investment) that your coaching provides.

- **For Permission:** Paint the future results of the coaching and highlight the benefits. Ask if you were granted permission would you want to proceed with this coaching program? This can often ascertain whether this is a genuine objection or not.
- **For Time**: Highlight the efficiencies and life improvements that clients can gain, ultimately freeing up more of their time.
- **For Value**: Use testimonials and case studies to demonstrate the tangible benefits your coaching has provided to others.
- **For Commitment**: Provide a lower commitment offering, like a single trial session or a shorter program, to help them ease into the process.

When faced with objections:

- Agree with them (e.g., "It is too expensive.")
- Ask for clarification. ("What does that mean for you?")
- "How do you feel about it? Where do you want to go from here?"
- "Would you like to discuss it further?"

The "Feel-Felt-Found" Method

This technique involves validating the client's **feelings**, sharing an example of someone who **felt** the same way and then describing how that person **found** value in overcoming that initial objection.

"I understand how you feel about the cost. I've had clients who felt the same way, but they found that the value and transformation they experienced far exceeded the initial investment."

Once you have addressed the objection, summarise what was discussed and ask for the client's feedback. This ensures that both parties are on the same page and solidifies the understanding reached during the discussion. It is essential to give the client some space to process the information you have presented. Do not rush into the next part of your sales pitch. Instead, a moment of pause can signify respect for their thought process and can often lead to the client convincing themselves of the value you are offering. This delicate balance of pacing, summarising and asking for feedback creates an environment where objections become stepping stones to a deeper understanding and a stronger client-coach relationship.

Building Trust

Building trust is the cornerstone of overcoming objections and fostering a strong coaching relationship. Trust is not something that is generally established fast. By showing respect and not rushing your client, you can often create meaningful interactions more quickly. Having a genuine commitment to the client's well-being, rather than being transactional, will shine through.

- **Transparency**: Be clear about your methods, what you offer and how you can assist in their personal or professional growth.

- **Empathy**: Show that you understand their objections and are there to help, not to push a sale.

- **Consistency**: Regular check-ins and follow-ups show you are not just there for the sale but for their ongoing development.

Combining these elements helps solidify a foundation of trust, making it easier to address and overcome any objections that may arise. After all, a client is more likely to listen to someone they trust, and trust is often the key variable that turns a sceptical prospect into a committed client. Always make trust building a core aspect of your coaching business strategy. It will set the stage for a long-term, productive relationship with each client you serve.

Dealing with Unresolvable Objections

It is essential to recognise that not all objections can or should be overcome. Some may signal that the client is not the right fit for your coaching service, and that's okay. In such cases, parting on amicable terms leaves the door open for future engagements or referrals.

Turning "No" Into "Yes" for Client Success

By proactively addressing objections and building a trust-based relationship with your clients, you are not just selling a service; you are promoting a transformative journey. Converting objections into affirmations is a skill that will both benefit your business and enable you to better serve your clients' needs. And ultimately, is not that why we became coaches in the first place?

Arming yourself with a deep understanding of these objections will enable you to answer your potential clients' queries more effectively and provide them with the clarity they need to make an informed decision. Remember, your goal is to guide them towards recognising their own needs and how your coaching services can fulfill them.

"Treat objections as requests for further information."
Brian Tracy

Activity, Should You Choose to Accept!

Objections are a normal part of doing business. Practice how to handle them.

1. **Practice "Feel-Felt-Found".**
   I understand how you feel about…
   I had a client that felt that way.
   What they found was…

Is "No" the Best Thing for Your Client?

It was a beautiful sunny day in a small farming town. The weather was so amazing that a few of the townsfolk got together to suggest they all go on holiday early that year. On the agreed day they all met at the town square ready to travel to the beach in convoy for their month's summer holiday.

Their cars packed, they were just about to leave when they realised someone was missing.

"Where is William?" Joe, William's neighbour asked.

Maybe he was late or had forgotten what day it was.

It was a short drive back to William's orchard, so Joe volunteered to go back and check on William.

When Joe arrived at William's orchard, William was hard at work picking apples.

"Come on, William!" he said. "It is such nice weather, now is the time to enjoy life! Put down your baskets and get in the van!"

"When the harvest is finished, I will take my holiday," William said.

Disappointed, Joe returned back to the town square, and everyone headed off without William.

One month later, after having had an incredible beachside holiday, they returned home.

What a sight they saw: all the apples were spoilt, on the ground, bird-pecked and rotting. They had nothing to eat, nothing to sell, and nothing to do. All the villagers were the same except for William.

William had picked all his produce, sold some and stored some for eating and seed saving. From his profits, he had enough left to book himself a lovely beach house for a month.

William's story offers an insightful angle to overcoming objections.

While the townsfolk had their objections to working during what seemed like the perfect time for a holiday, William navigated through the short-term allure to focus on his long-term goals. It is easy to say "no" because it feels like the less risky option, a way to avoid failing to meet expectations, either our own or those of others. Your clients' objections are often signposts pointing to deeper concerns or priorities, not barriers to be avoided. Your client is often offering you a chance to explain your solution more clearly. William shows us that saying "no" to immediate temptations and overcoming the objections of the community allows us the freedom to say "yes" to more substantial, long-lasting rewards. In sales conversations, just as in life, "no" is often a placeholder for "I'm not sure," and it is your role to guide the dialogue towards a more informed "yes" or a true "no"!

Looking after your clients is only one part of your business. If you don't look after yourself, you won't have a business. Now you have overcome the objection, you need to look after your well-being too. Let's go on to Chapter 11.

Chapter 11

Balancing Your Coaching Life for Long Term Success

Running a successful coaching practice is not just about acquiring clients and delivering excellent service; it is also about managing yourself. Time and energy are your most valuable assets, and how you manage them will largely dictate your level of success and well-being. Balancing your professional life for long-term success is a must to create a thriving business year after year.

Overcoming Self-Doubt

In addition to managing your time and energy, overcoming self-doubt is another essential aspect of maintaining a balanced and successful coaching practice. Doubts and uncertainties can plague even the most seasoned professionals. Whether it is the common fear of inadequacy known as Imposter Syndrome or simply questioning the value you bring to your clients, it is critical to recognise these negative thought patterns. Actively challenging these doubts strengthens your mental resilience and enhances your effectiveness as a coach. Learning to trust yourself can empower you to make wiser business decisions, deepen your client relationships and, ultimately, cultivate a coaching practice that stands the test of time.

Imposter Syndrome

It is real. Imposter Syndrome is a psychological pattern where you doubt your skills, talents or accomplishments, often feeling like a fraud despite evidence of your competence. This syndrome can be particularly debilitating in a coaching setting, where your clients look to you for guidance and expertise. It is essential to remember that even the most accomplished professionals experience these feelings at some point. Rather than let it undermine your confidence and impact your performance, use it as a catalyst for continued learning and improvement. Recognising that Imposter Syndrome is a shared human experience, rather than a reflection of your actual abilities, can be a crucial step in moving past self-doubt and providing the quality of service that you are fully capable of delivering.

Go to my podcast, *Small Business Talk for Coaches*, to listen to more tips on overcoming Imposter Syndrome. The episodes are listed in the resources at the end of this chapter.

Time Management Techniques

The key to successful time management is having the right systems in place. With that foundation, you can more effectively implement strategies to organise your day. Having these systems and strategies fine-tuned allows you to focus on what truly matters in your coaching business, from client engagement to personal development. Here are a few options to try:

- **Time Blocking:** Dedicate blocks of time in your day for specific activities, such as client meetings, marketing, and personal development. Consistency is key here.

- **The Pomodoro Technique:** Work in bursts of 25 minutes, followed by a 5-minute break. This can improve your concentration and productivity.

- **The Eisenhower Matrix:** Classify tasks into four categories: urgent and important, important but not urgent, urgent but not important and neither. This helps in prioritising your tasks more effectively.

- **Batching:** Group similar tasks together to perform them sequentially without interruption. This reduces the mental load of switching between different types of activities.

I love The Pomodoro Technique, using 50-minute work sprints followed by a 10-minute break, during which I usually do 250 steps and try to go outside. My home office desk is right beside the kitchen, so I use the oven timer, which is very annoying and doesn't stop until you turn it off.

Prioritising Tasks

Prioritisation is pivotal for productive time management. To excel in this, there are several tried and true methods that can help you identify what tasks to tackle first, thereby maximising your efficiency and overall impact. Here are some strategies:

- The ABCDE Method:

    It is straightforward yet a very effective way to prioritise your tasks.

    Label each task on your to-do list with a letter from A to E, where A represents the most critical tasks that require immediate attention, and E marks the least important.

    Once you have categorised your tasks, start by completing all the "A" tasks before moving on to "B" tasks, and so on. This method helps you focus on what really matters and ensures that you are spending your time and energy on tasks that will have the most significant impact on your business.

- The 80/20 Rule, also known as the Pareto Principle.

    The idea is that a small chunk of what you do ends up making a big difference in your results. In the context of marketing for your coaching business, it means that a minority of your activities will generate most of your results.

For example, you might find that only 20% of your marketing channels bring in 80% of your clients. Or a few of your service offerings generate the bulk of your income. By identifying these high-impact activities, you can prioritise your time and resources more effectively. Instead of spreading yourself thin across multiple areas, you can concentrate on the activities that truly matter and are likely to bring in the most returns.

Focus on the 20% of activities that will yield 80% of your results. This approach will not only make you more productive, but also enhance the efficiency and profitability of your business.

- The MoSCoW Method: Categorise tasks into Must-haves, Should-haves, Could-haves, and Won't-haves.

This method is another practical way to categorise and prioritise your tasks.

Divide your tasks into 4 four categories:

1. Must-haves
2. Should-haves
3. Could-haves
4. Won't-haves.

Must-haves are tasks that are non-negotiable and need to be completed as soon as possible. Should-haves are important but not urgent and can be scheduled for a later time if needed. Could-haves are tasks that would be nice to complete but are not critical for your immediate success. Finally, Won't-haves are tasks that you can safely ignore or defer indefinitely without any negative impact on your business.

By applying the MoSCoW Method, you can quickly identify which tasks deserve your immediate attention and which can wait, helping you manage your time more effectively.

- Setting Boundaries: Be clear about what you can realistically achieve and learn to say no when necessary. Overcommitting dilutes the quality of your work and can lead to burnout.

Avoiding Burnout

Coaching is an emotionally demanding profession that requires a great deal of mental and emotional energy to truly engage with clients and help them navigate their challenges. This intensity can make burnout a very real possibility if you are not careful about managing your own well-being in addition to your clients'. Therefore, it is essential to implement self-care strategies to maintain your resilience and effectiveness as a coach.

- **Scheduled Downtime:** Mark time in your calendar for rest and relaxation. Whether it is a hobby, spending time with loved ones or simply doing nothing, this time is crucial for your mental health.

- **Work-Life Balance:** Make sure to carve out time for your personal life. Maintaining a healthy work-life balance keeps you energised and focused when you are working.

- **Exercise:** Incorporate physical exercise into your routine to release stress, improve your mood and enhance your overall physical health. Exercise is a powerful tool for combating burnout and should be an integral part of your self-care strategy.

- **Regular Self-Assessment:** Periodically assess your workload, stress levels and general well-being. Use these assessments to make adjustments to your routine as needed.

- **Seek Support:** Don't hesitate to consult mentors, colleagues or even mental health professionals to help you navigate stress and avoid burnout.

Are You Self-Sabotaging Your Own Success?

Often, you may sabotage your own success without even realising it, and certainly not with any intention to do so. Subconsciously, you could find yourself damaging or interrupting your own progress before reaping any rewards. Sometimes it might seem easier to let yourself fail rather than put in the necessary work to succeed and realise your dreams. At other times, fear of what success could actually entail may hold you back, even if this fear operates at a subconscious level.

- All rich people are mean.
- Successful business owners have no time for their families.
- You can't be a good Mum and have a successful business.
- You can't have it all.
- People like *you* have to work hard.

Have you ever said or heard any of these?

Think about the ones you tell yourself. What stories are you telling yourself so that you don't have to get out of your comfort zone?

Confronting the root causes of self-sabotage is essential. Understanding why you self-sabotage, is a critical step in breaking this detrimental cycle. Often, these self-defeating behaviours are deeply ingrained, stemming from past experiences, societal narratives or even from family beliefs passed down through generations. These limiting beliefs can form a mental script that dictates your actions, keeping you in a perpetual state of stagnation or even decline. To tackle self-sabotage, it is important to identify these hidden triggers and confront them head-on.

Whether it is fear of success, fear of failure or the notion that you don't deserve success, these underlying issues need to be addressed. Doing so not only liberates you from self-imposed barriers but also paves the way for a more fulfilling and sustainable coaching career. Take some time to introspect and maybe even seek external perspectives, be it through mentorship or professional guidance, to uncover the reasons behind your self-sabotaging behaviours. Only then can you truly free yourself and set the stage for long-term success.

Continual Learning and Your Coaching Practice

Continual learning is a cornerstone of any successful coaching practice. The coaching industry is dynamic, constantly evolving with new methodologies, tools and client expectations. To remain relevant and effective, it is imperative to invest in ongoing education. This does not mean just acquiring new coaching techniques. You also need to stay abreast of trends in marketing, technology and even psychology that could impact your practice. Whether you attend workshops, take online courses or simply read up on the latest research, ongoing learning ensures that you are offering the best possible service to your clients. It keeps you competitive and allows you to adapt to the ever-changing landscape of coaching, enriching both your business and the lives of those you help.

While continuous learning is crucial, it is important not to use the pursuit of extra qualifications as a form of procrastination. Acquiring endless certificates without implementing what you have learned does not serve you or your clients. The key is to strike a balance between educational growth and practical application. This will ensure that each new skill or piece of knowledge you acquire is integrated into your coaching practice for tangible results.

Balancing Your Coaching Life for Long-Term Success

You have got this!

It is essential to strike a sustainable balance between your coaching practice and personal well-being. A balanced life will be beneficial for you and enhance the quality of the service you provide to your clients. Success in coaching is not a sprint; it is a marathon that requires steady, sustained effort over the long term.

> *"At the end of the day, you are the only one that is limiting your ability to dream or to actually execute on your dreams. Don't let yourself get in the way of that."*
> *Falon Fatemi*

Activity, Should You Choose to Accept!

Make your well-being a priority, no matter how busy you get.

1. **Implement Some of the Strategies Listed.**
   Pick one and start there.

2. **Listen to these podcast episodes:**
   You might like to listen to my podcast at https://SmallBusinessTalk.com.au or on your favourite podcast app. Try these episodes to start with:

   #12 Impostor Syndrome, what is it and do you have it?
   #23 How Imposter Syndrome Could Be Holding Your Business Back with Katrina Alilovic
   #36 Work-Life balance – Is it a myth, a fairytale, you can't really have it all.
   #181 What If You Could?

Are Limiting Beliefs Holding You Back?

Mark got a summer job leading elephants around his local town for tourists.

On his first day, he noticed that none of the elephants were caged or restrained for the night. Instead, they were all housed in a paddock with a single rope tied around one ankle of each animal. Checking the rope confirmed that it was just ordinary rope, nothing that could hold an elephant if it wanted to escape.

"Aren't you worried they will get free?" he asked his coworker, Brian.

"No," Brian said. "Watch them. They don't even try."

Sure enough, Brian was right.

"Are the elephants sick?" Mark asked his boss when they arrived the next morning.

"No, why?" the boss said.

"None of the elephants try to escape," Mark said.

"No, they don't know they can. They just think they are helpless. You see, when the elephants are very young, we tie a piece of rope around their ankle. They pull on it, but they can't get it off because as babies they are too small. They try for a few days and then realise they can't do it and never try again. So even now they have grown up, they don't try because they believe that the rope is stronger than they are."

Is not it fascinating how a simple rope can hold back such a powerful animal, simply because it believes it is unable to break free?

This story serves as a powerful metaphor for the mental barriers and limiting beliefs that can hold you back in your coaching career.

Whether it is

- self-doubt
- imposter syndrome
- time management
- self-sabotage

Or societal narratives that have been ingrained in you, these "ropes" can keep you confined in a paddock of your own making. It is essential to examine these beliefs critically, challenge them and find a way to cut the rope. By doing so, you will not only liberate yourself but also set the stage for a more balanced, successful and sustainable coaching practice.

You are almost there. Here is Chapter 12. The last chapter. Now your journey really begins.

Chapter 12

Your Roadmap to Mapping a Thriving Coaching Business

The road to a successful coaching business is rarely smooth. Navigating the path from attracting potential clients to retaining loyal ones is both an art and a science. By understanding where to find clients, mastering your marketing funnel, building lasting relationships and delivering an unmatched client experience, you will set yourself up for a long-term thriving business in the competitive world of coaching.

You may encounter objections when you are doing a consult or asking for a sale. These objections are a natural part of the decision-making process. How you handle these objections can significantly influence the success of your business.

A successful coaching practice is not just about gaining clients and offering first-class service; it is also about self-management. Your time and energy are fundamental assets that influence both your success and well-being. Striking a professional balance is essential for sustained business growth.

Common Coaching Mistakes to Avoid

Here are some frequent mistakes that coaches make, which can hinder growth and their future success:

1. Not defining a niche.
2. Not having a clear message.
3. Not believing in themselves and telling people.
4. Not running their practice as a REAL Business.
5. Allowing FEAR (False Evidence Appearing Real) to control their actions.
6. Not understanding that Price = Value.
7. Not taking action and marketing.
8. Not having a consistent plan.
9. Not making it clear to potential clients what you sell or how to buy it from you.
10. Not dealing with setbacks and allowing small things to derail your business journey.

Navigating the complexities of a coaching business can be challenging, but remember, you have got this. You are a fabulous coach, equipped with the skills and passion to make a meaningful impact.

Your Roadmap to Mapping a Thriving Coaching Business

Congratulations on making it to the end of this comprehensive guide! You have navigated through the important aspects of establishing, running and scaling a coaching business. Let's quickly recap what you have learned.

Defining Your Coaching Niche: "How to Stand Out on the Coaching Map"

Starting off strong, you learned the importance of deciding on a niche to make your mark. We explored how to identify your target audience and match your skills and passions to their needs.

Building a Strong Brand Identity: "Crafting an Identity Beyond the Certificate"

Moving from the niche, we focused on the elements that make you uniquely you. Your brand identity. You learned how to see yourself as a coach and to articulate this vision through compelling brand messages and an effective online presence.

Branding: "Turning Identity into a Brand"

Here, we looked at the tangible aspects of your brand, from logo design to marketing your brand in actionable ways.

Creating Your Coaching Program: "Your Powerful Coaching Toolbox"

Once your brand is firmly in place, we explored how to construct a coaching program that serves your clients' needs. You got insights into types of programs, structuring your sessions and setting measurable goals.

Setting the Right Price: "Setting Your Price for Success"

You looked into the financial side, learning how to price your services effectively. From various pricing models to calculating your worth and tackling pricing objections, you learned the business side of coaching.

Understanding Marketing Channels: "Laying the Groundwork to Your Ideal Audience"

This chapter set the stage for your marketing strategy by helping you explore various marketing channels suitable for your niche.

Marketing Strategies for Success: "Marketing Magic to Find Clients Who Love You"

We then tackled the art of marketing in detail, helping you construct a robust marketing plan and measure its effectiveness.

Sales Techniques for Coaches: "Mastering the Art of Client Conversion"

Next, we switched gears to the sales process, equipping you with tools to handle sales conversations and overcome hurdles.

Client Attraction: "Magnetising Your Ideal Client"

In this chapter, we focused on ways to attract your ideal clients, the importance of understanding the sales funnel tailored for coaches and how to make that initial contact that sets the stage for a long-term relationship.

Overcoming Objections: "Turning 'No' Into 'Yes' for Client Success"

Here, you learned how to turn challenges into opportunities by understanding common objections in coaching and effective strategies to overcome them.

Managing Your Time and Energy: "Balancing Your Coaching Life for Long-Term Success"

Finally, you learned how to manage your time and energy to prevent burnout and maintain a healthy work-life balance, which is crucial for long term success. You are the most important asset in your business.

Armed with this knowledge, you are now fully prepared to embark on or continue your coaching journey with greater clarity, confidence and purpose. Best of luck in your endeavours, and remember, the road to success is always under construction. Keep building!

Here are some key takeaways that encapsulate the core principles and strategies from this guide:

1. **Niche Specialisation:** Don't try to be a coach for everyone; focus on a specific target audience where you can provide the most value.

2. **Brand Identity:** Understand that your brand is more than just a logo or a certificate; it is the emotional and psychological relationship you have with your clients.

3. **Coaching Program Structure:** Offer a coaching program that is effective and client focused, tailored to meet the unique needs and goals of your client.

4. **Pricing Strategy:** Price your services based on value, and be prepared to effectively address any objections or queries around pricing.

5. **Marketing Know How:** Utilise a variety of channels to attract clients; it is not a one-size-fits-all approach.

6. **Sales Conversion:** Move beyond the notion of "selling" to a more relational approach, where you are guiding your prospective clients towards making an informed decision.

7. **Client Retention:** Building relationships is key to retaining clients. Maintain contact and provide value even after the sales process.

8. **Overcoming Objections:** Learning how to handle objections effectively can turn potential "Nos" into definite "Yeses".

9. **Managing Time and Energy:** Prioritise your tasks effectively to avoid burnout and to ensure that you are always performing at your best for your clients.

10. **Continual Learning:** The coaching industry is always evolving; keep updating your skills and knowledge to remain relevant and effective.

These takeaways will serve as a quick reference guide and a reminder of the important facets that contribute to a successful coaching business.

Next Steps

To further elevate your coaching business:

1. **Implement What You've Learned**: Take the insights and strategies from this guide and the courses to refine your approach, from attracting clients to retaining them, so you can run a more efficient and effective coaching business.

2. **Visit CathySmith.com.au**: Start by visiting the website for exclusive content, tips and strategies tailored for coaches who are passionate about transforming their coaching skills into a thriving business.

3. **Enrol in the Coaches Marketing Roadmap Course**: Take this journey alongside other aspiring coaches and benefit from structured learning. This course will walk you through the process of turning your coaching skills into a successful business, providing you with all the tools you need.

By taking these steps and engaging with the resources available through Cathy Smith Coaching, you will be well on your way to turning your coaching passion into a thriving, profitable business.

Congratulations, Coach.

Be a fabulous coach, make lots of money and do good in the world.

Cathy Smith

About the Author

Cathy Smith was born in Victoria and moved to Western Australia at age 7 when her parents bought a house in the South West, during a family holiday. As a young girl, Cathy loved returning to Melbourne to spend time with her grandparents, and that was where her love of design and travel was fostered. Cathy's passion for design turned into a love of marketing when she became a mother and decided to start her own business instead of returning to her corporate job in 2001. After working with small business owners for 20 years, Cathy expanded her expertise by adding personal and business coaching qualifications to her business and marketing skills. She thought she would get a qualification for the consultancy work that she had been doing for all those years. Little did she know! Coaching became Cathy's new love, and seeing new coaches struggling to build a business from their coaching, she knew helping them thrive would be her next passion.

In 1990, Cathy moved back to Melbourne, where she lived and worked for 2 years. She then embarked on a 3-month Australian holiday, which unexpectedly turned into a 15-year working adventure via North Queensland. She now lives back in Western Australia's beautiful south coast with her husband, dog and chooks. She can often be seen walking around the garden, getting her steps up or enjoying a well-brewed cup of Earl Grey tea. In her spare time, Cathy loves spending time at the beach, gardening, travelling or with her family.

Testimonials

"The Coaches Marketing Roadmap was right place, right time for me. I had been struggling for a while to find a presence as a coach but definitely found it in the Coaches Marketing Roadmap. The unique combination of the weekly group discussions that Cathy was able to coach and personalise to our own particular situations, followed by the mentoring of then "how" to market this to our own particular targeted audience has been brilliant.

Through the Coaches Marketing Roadmap I was able to find the clarity, confidence and direction I was looking for in regards to what my coaching stood for and how I could represent and now market that and myself as a coaching business the way I have always wanted, and I thoroughly recommend Cathy and her program to anyone looking to do the same."

Graeme Willox

"Cathy is awesome. there's not really much else to be said. She's helped me find my purpose and allowed me to be more focused on getting results from my business. Highly recommended!"

David Ucyurek

"Cathy is a great coach and highly recommended. She has helped me transition through a tough time in my life."

Alex

"Cathy is a remarkable coach! Her marketing knowledge, systems and approach helps you achieve real results for your business. If you're looking to grow your business and/or expand your client base, she is absolutely the coach to work with—I can't recommend her highly enough!"

Laurene McKenzie

"Cathy Smith is an articulate and sophisticated communicator with a natural flare for public speaking and of course, leadership. She genuinely cares about helping her clients produce their best possible results, and she always has a positive attitude with a warm ear to ear smile! Thank you, Cathy, for all that you do".

Carlos Garcia

Cathy Smith

COACHES MARKETING ROADMAP

Speaking Topics

How to Stand Out on the Coaching Map

Crafting an Identity Beyond a Coaching Certificate

Marketing Magic to Find Clients Who Love You

Mastering the Art of Client Conversion

A Roadmap to Creating a Thriving Coaching Business

Cathy Smith is an inspiring speaker, acclaimed author, and marketing expert with over 35 years in the industry. As the author of the **Coaches Marketing Roadmap,** she's a leading authority in coaching and marketing, dedicated to helping coaches build successful businesses. Her approach blends traditional marketing with digital-age strategies, proven in her work with hundreds of businesses to enhance their brand and audience reach.

The **Coaches Marketing Roadmap** distils Cathy's vast experience into practical strategies for coaches at all levels, lauded for its real-world applicability and empathetic guidance. Known for her engaging, clear, and relatable style, Cathy's workshops and keynotes are interactive and empowering, enabling attendees to immediately apply their learnings. Her contributions have made her a sought-after consultant and speaker in coaching and marketing communities.

coach@cathysmith.com.au
cathysmith.com.au

Acknowledgements

Thank you to everyone who has been part of this journey.

Special thanks to Lyn Hawkins for starting my coaching journey and to Kathy McKenzie, an incredible coach, mentor, and facilitator, who allows us all to thrive. Kylie Stewart for being an amazing coach, mentor, facilitator and friend. Craig Levitt for being the wonderful coach, mentor, and facilitator that you are. Steve Taylor, for all your encouragement.

Mike Cameron, for reigniting the book dream.

Heartfelt gratitude to Kyle Spyrides for endless support and inspiration, and to Alex Ironside for encouraging me to stay up. Tami Pritchard and Stuart Denman for helping to bring the dream to reality.

To my coaching buddies—Graeme Willox, Peter Dijkema, Kerrie Nobes, Jeannette White, Shelly Flett, Lyn Hawkins, Lisa Targett, and Stephen Heinz—you have been invaluable in my coaching journey. To Janet Dunbar-Smith for being such a wonderful friend and allowing me to attend networking events in the beginning.

A special mention to Graeme Willox and Harvey Knopman, the first participants of the Coaches Marketing Roadmap, whose involvement was crucial in bringing this book to life. To Kylie Stewart, Emma Malica and Stephen Heinz for reading my manuscript and for your invaluable comments and suggestions. To my editor Marnae Kelley for your tireless hours reading and proofing.

To all my clients, for all the knowledge and learnings that I have gained over the last 22 years, you have shaped my business journey in innumerable ways. To my dedicated staff, your hard work and years of service have been the backbone of our success.

To my Husband, and family, you are my everything—the support and love you have provided are the foundation of all my activities.

www.ingramcontent.com/pod-product-compliance
Lightning Source LLC
Chambersburg PA
CBHW030038100526
44590CB00011B/257